MICHAEL BURGE is an Australian journalist and writer who was born at Inverell in the New England region of NSW. He grew up in the Blue Mountains, lived in England for most of the 1990s, and now resides on Coochiemudlo Island in Queensland's Moreton Bay with his husband and their two dogs.

TITLES BY MICHAEL BURGE

Fiction

Closet His, Closet Hers

Literary non-fiction

Merely Players: Acting like Shakespeare really matters

Non-fiction

Questionable Deeds: Making a stand for equal love

Pluck: Exploits of the single-minded

Write, Regardless! A no-nonsense guide to plotting,
packaging & promoting your book

Plays

Merely Players

For information about upcoming titles go to
www.burgewords.com

WRITE, REGARDLESS!

*A no-nonsense guide to plotting,
packaging & promoting your book*

MICHAEL BURGE

*'The doing of something productive regardless
of the outcome is an act of faith.'*

Julia Cameron

First published in Australia in 2016 by www.burgewords.com
Copyright © Michael Burge 2016

National Library of Australia
Cataloguing-in-Publication data:

Title: Write, Regardless! A no-nonsense guide to plotting, packaging
& marketing your book / Michael Burge.

ISBN: 9780994388773 (paperback)

Subjects: Writing--Handbooks, manuals, etc.
Authorship--Handbooks, manuals, etc.
Authorship--Marketing--Handbooks, manuals, etc
Authors and publishers--Handbooks, manuals, etc.

Dewey Number: 070.5

Contents

Foreword

WRITERS ARE LIVING through tough times, and times are usually tough enough for wordsmiths.

Not since the invention of the printing press has it been easier to publish books using an array of affordable online publishing services, but these same systems and the distribution networks they feed have stripped the traditional currency of many of the same books to almost nothing.

Newspapers struggle to get readers to pay, and we now have multiple generations who do not expect any content should come with a price tag.

Yet it's not all bad news. Despite the terrible odds stacked up against writing for fame, glory and riches, people still tell stories.

My lack of success in landing a traditional publishing contract for my work led me down this pathway, even as a log-jam of manuscripts was piling up in my head, heart and hard-drive. *Write, Regardless!* is the result of having many questions fired at me ever since I threw my cap in the ring and became a publisher who made a small splash.

I once worked in publishing and learned a thing or two about gauging what makes a good story, a savvy author and a win-win contract, but I needed to spend years researching online processes and social media in order to lay the foundations for this step into the partially-unknown.

And I hasten to add I don't have the answer every question. I'm still learning, but after finding myself corresponding at length about my approach, and thereby losing time for my own work, I decided to look at how I achieved my limited success in order to have somewhere to direct queries.

In my first year as an independent publisher I profited from the publication of four titles, which made money after significant sales to libraries of the paperback version of my strongest non-fiction title *Questionable Deeds: Making a stand for equal love*. This title had relevance to the news cycle in that it spoke considerably to the critical political journey of marriage equality legislation in Australia.

The publication of *Closet His, Closet Hers: Collected stories* at the same time was no mistake. Fiction is a much harder sell, and I consciously floated my first fictional title on the same wave as *Questionable Deeds*. To put it plainly, I was objective enough to make decisions as a publisher as much as I was making them as a writer.

That is the key to *Write, Regardless!* It seeks to unlock publishing industry secrets, but it will also raise your awareness of what it takes to spend your precious time writing *regardless* of what the publishing industry thinks of all your hard work.

This book is not aimed at teaching you to write, although it has several encouragements to analyse your work to make it more engaging and entertaining to readers. It doesn't offer short cuts. I started creating an online presence as a journalist twelve months before I started writing my first published book, and I encourage readers to give the process at least the same time as I have, which is now approaching five years.

Writing is about doing the work. Publishing is about even harder work. Marketing and promoting a book is the hardest work most independent publishers will ever do.

Write, Regardless! is the technique I applied to myself, and in doing so earned a third of a traditionally published writer's average annual salary in my first year, without any support whatsoever from the traditional publishing industry or the mainstream media.

That might sound like very small fry, but weighed up with the high chance of getting ripped off thousands of dollars for the 'one-stop-shop' charlatans, or outsourcing the work to others, it's a resounding success story. I made more than many authors receive from books that have been treated to the full suite of marketing and promotion, festivals and competitions.

As I write this, I am preparing to attend my first writers event as part of a panel discussion at Brisbane Writers Festival. For a self-published author in any country that is almost unheard of.

Write, Regardless! is available free online as a series of articles on my website, but I'm publishing it here with all the same links to other resources I created on the journey.

It will be of optimal use to writers who have at least one manuscript completed and the willingness to create another with a regular writing schedule of no less than a page of new material a week. It's also designed for you to begin the work of becoming a publisher at the end of each chapter, before moving onto the next.

One page a week sounds like a small amount, but there is more to being an author than writing these days. Read on and courageously *do the work!*

Michael Burge, 2016.

Is Write, Regardless! for me?

I SPENT OVER six years writing full time, including three years contributing online articles, before embarking on the publication of a line of titles across 2015-2016, books I wrote while developing a social media readership. The *Write, Regardless!* series of no-nonsense articles explains how I went from a good writer, to an Amazon bestselling* author (without getting ripped off along the way).

Write, Regardless! **is for you if:**

You can write. I don't believe anyone can teach us how, but all writers can learn how to write better articles, short stories, novels, journalism, non-fiction, poetry and memoir, and to enter the publishing industry at the right time and in the right shape.

You want to create a place for readers to access your entire body of work.

You have an 'embarrassing' manuscript tucked away in a desk drawer or buried on your computer desktop, and you want to turn it into a viable publication.

You want to learn how to approach traditional publishers and literary agents before trying self publishing.

You want to learn about plotting better story arcs, copy editing and proofreading your own work, designing effective book covers and marketing books independently.

You want to learn how to set up an effective social media platform without spending much money.

Your pile of rejection letters from traditional publishers is getting so thick you're considering self publishing.

You want to self publish without getting ripped off.

You want to manage the self publication process yourself and learn how to communicate effectively with publishing support creatives such as editors and designers, in order to get the best finished product.

I'll be honest and upfront in these posts. I'll also keep things light, because I have just finished publishing some very serious books, and I need a lift! I'll link to Wikipedia quite often, so if you don't like updated, peer-reviewed, democratised information, *Write, Regardless!* is definitely not for you.

Wikipedia? Are you being serious? I regularly consult Wikipedia because many online entities don't really want us to know exactly how they work (so they can charge us money). At Wikipedia, other people have spent time sharing how things work, and I'm assuming you've got enough of a bullshit monitor that if someone hacked Wikipedia and posted: "Marilyn Monroe was actually a donkey", you'd work out they're trying to trick you, right?

Writer, identify yourself!

IF YOU DON'T identify yourself as a writer, no-one will do it for you. Hopefully you're coming with me on the crazy ride that the *Write, Regardless!* series will be, aimed at anyone who can write, or perhaps has a 'embarrassing' manuscript sitting in a desk draw or on a computer somewhere. The reason that manuscript remains unpublished is not the sick, sad, selfish world, but because you have not published it yet. Time to get real, join the publishing industry, and do it yourself. Many thousands of successful writers have taken this path before you. Many have been ripped off by charlatans, and I am here to help us avoid that.

Don't start by writing anything

Writing is way down on the list of jobs you need to start doing. I'll assume you know how, have some work under your belt, and a regular writing schedule. Your first task is to identify yourself so readers can find you. There are a few ways to do this. The ones I know about are Gravatar and Google. Because you are the best spokesperson of your work, in fact probably its only spokesperson, eventually you'll want readers to find you.

Gravatar is good

A 'globally recognised avatar' does a really cool thing – wherever you participate on the internet, a Gravatar lets your identity follow you, and if people like the comment you made on *The Huffington Post*, they'll be able to find your website, and therefore maybe get interested in your writing. That's called being discoverable. If you'd rather hide behind a name like 'Hawkwind Gamester of the Windy Witches' and have no identifiable online presence, go for it, but best put that name on all your books, not your real name. If you want people to start identifying and understanding you, and therefore your books, get a free Gravatar account today, with a real headshot of yourself. Gravatar accounts go hand in hand with WordPress websites (more on those in coming chapters).

Google is good

A few years ago, Google got even savvier than it already was and allowed people access to a Google account linked to all kinds of portals, including Blogger (the alternative to WordPress for website hosting). The best part about a Google account is it lets Google know what you're up to. Don't be scared! Telling the world's largest online information aggregator what you're up to is called publicity, essential for publishing (see what I did there? The root word is the same in publish, publicity, publication... your *public*, darling). Sign up for a free Google account.

Set and forget your Google and Gravatar accounts

You're not going to need to go in and out of these places very often (phew). Eventually I'll explain how to update them automatically without leaving your website. For now, the only other thing to do is to keep a list of your account names and passwords. Keep them somewhere safe and accessible.

Keeping online platforms in their place

Online platforms will continually promote 'bells and whistles' (attractive additional features or trimmings). Very often, they'll try to trick you into thinking you need 'premium' products, or provide extra information like your email address or your mobile phone number, in order to increase your security levels or to maximise your visibility. I have the most basic accounts on Twitter, Facebook, LinkedIn, Storify, Google, SoundCloud, YouTube, Canva, Ingram Spark, Amazon Author Central (don't freak out at this list, I will explain them all in future articles) Gravatar and MailChimp, and until recently the free WordPress account, which I upgraded only so I could host video/audio marketing content. Stay on your guard when navigating online platforms.

Don't click 'yes' unless you're sure you have to. 'Cancel' or 'skip' buttons are best unless you're 100 per cent sure you want to alter something.

Sharing information

Online platforms will sometimes ask your permission to share your information with your followers, which you'll want to do, since it's these networks of friends, family and interested people who are our readership base. Say yes to those prompts, it's simply a legal requirement of the platform to ask.

Internet fears

The internet can be a big scary place, and rip-off merchants are out there, sure, but I have not come across any real monsters. The only times I have wasted money on my publishing journey was through being ill-informed. The main internet shenanigans I see are the corporate obstacles that big companies place in the way of their competition, and sometimes writers have our pathways impacted by these shifts that are out of our control. Move bravely between giants!

Recap

Get your free Gravatar and Google accounts sorted, start a safe place for usernames and passwords, then get on with your day job secure in the knowledge that the internet now knows who you are. Don't be scared, because that means readers! (*Whoosh!* There go your internet fears!).

Writer, show off your assets!

IT'S NOT TIME for writers to stress about our writing (there'll be hours of that later) just keep up a regular writing schedule and start creating social media assets. These are tools such as WordPress, Twitter, Facebook, LinkedIn, Goodreads and others which allow us to interact with other social media users and – importantly for writers – for readers to find and follow us to access our books.

Why do I need social media assets?

The social media has become the greatest shop window for writing the world has ever seen. Having multiple social media assets also increases a writer's 'search engine optimisation' (SEO) – your ranking on search results via search engines like Google.

Web of Fabulousness

By creating a cluster of social media assets using your real name, you are telling the internet you exist. As search engines aggregate information about you, they'll notice you more when your name pops up on Facebook and Twitter and other social media sites. I call this a writer's Web of Fabulousness as it nets followers naturally (without you having to buy them).

Putting the 'social' in social media

Use your social media assets regularly. Read, share and

comment online just as you normally would. Participate! Remember, it's called the 'social' media. Like the level of socialisation that employees participate in at the coffee station, you share something, you learn something, and you're sociable, which means keeping yourself a bit nice. Don't do the hard sell, however. If someone's at the water cooler flogging their cleaning products every day, you'll avoid them, right? The key to social media participation is to do it genuinely without constant pressure to buy things.

Why is this essential for marketing?

Because these word-of-mouth moments are still the greatest form of promotion available, they are free, and many believe they are the only form of advertising that really works. If you want your work to find readers, participate in the social media.

Domain names don't matter

In the early years of the internet, everyone was focussed on domain names, and there's still a common fear that we need to buy a domain name before someone gets the one we want. While this used to be the case, it's no longer essential to have a domain name to market something. I am a writer called Michael Burge who lives on Coochiemudlo Island, and all my social media assets have my name, my vocation and my location embedded in them. If you google the terms: 'Writer', 'Michael' and 'Coochiemudlo', you'll find my website. If you google those terms and add 'Facebook' or 'Twitter', you'll find my website, Facebook and Twitter accounts in one search. You don't need to ensure people write down your domain name these days, just say: "Google 'Writer Michael Burge' and you'll find me!". Even if they forget half the details, they'll find you, thanks to what's known as metadata.

Metadata is what matters

Metadata describes something (e.g. a writer, or a book) and allows it to be found again by browsing or searching. In the blogging world, metadata has been filtered-down into a process of creating tags and categories for each page of information you publish on your website or blog. I participate in the social media with a special interest in LGBTIQ equality, so if you google my name and 'marriage equality' or 'LGBTIQ', you'll also find me, because I regularly use these terms as tags and categories. More on this process when we get to blogging. For now, let go of domain-name thinking, the world has moved on to metadata.

Usernames and User IDs

In order to generate good SEO and social media followings, using your real name is ideal for social media assets, however, in most cases your real name will already have been used by someone else. To counter this issue, social media platforms allow you to have a User ID, sometimes known as a 'handle', which is a form of nickname (for example, my Twitter handle and my WordPress URL both use 'burgewords'); leaving you to label your asset profile with your real name. Think of a simple, short word that describes what you do and that nobody else in the world is using, and consider this for your URL and social media username or User ID.

WordPress is the way

Every writer needs a website, an online place to showcase our work to the world, allowing readers to find our books, and public relations (PR) people and journalists, booksellers and book trade people to contact us. Creating a website was once an expensive business that many writers needed to pay someone to do for us, but since the advent of the world's largest blogging platforms, Blogger and WordPress, it's been possible to create a free blog that works as a website.

A blog (a 'web-log') is not for everyone. I have a WordPress blog platform which I use as a website, and for more than three years I had a basic, free, WordPress account, recently upgraded in order for me to host video marketing material for around USD$129 annually. Set up your free site with your service provider of choice – it will be a major tool in your writing journey, and it will evolve.

Since you already have a Gravatar account, setting up WordPress will be easy as the platforms are linked. Remember, if someone else is using your real name as their WordPress URL, think of an alternative name (like mine – 'burgewords') and use your real name as the profile User ID. The next chapter of *Write, Regardless!* is all about using a WordPress site.

Twitter is tops

Twitter is misunderstood. Before I was on it I believed it was the domain of navel gazers and people intent on telling me what it was like on the bus as they commuted... *boring!* It is all that, but used wisely, Twitter is also a fantastic distribution network for journalism, books and other publications.

Set up your free Twitter account, but remember, if someone else is using your real name as their Twitter handle, think of an alternative handle name (like mine, @burgewords) and use your real name as the profile User ID. Twitter will assist you to set up and start tweeting. Find my Twitter handle and follow me. I'll follow you back if you send me a tweet (learn how to 'tweet to' someone). More about using Twitter for marketing in a later chapter.

Facebook is fab

If you have a Facebook timeline (the basic Facebook account to keep tabs on your friends) you can also create a free Facebook Page. Facebook will ask you to identify the type of business you are.

Like me, the word 'business' might give you a jolt, but publishing your books will be a business, I assure you, so move past this with confidence. There is an option to select 'Writer'. My Facebook Page allows me to promote myself in all forms of writing – non-fiction, fiction, journalism and playwriting.

The benefit of having a Facebook Page (your business) in addition to your Facebook timeline (your personal life) is that it gives you a place specifically for communicating about your books to an interested following. There will be more about using Facebook for marketing later in *Write, Regardless!*

A LinkedIn your chain (see what I did there?)

LinkedIn is a bit strange to me as it's very corporate, but I embraced it as a social media asset simply because it adds to my Web of Fabulousness, and the basic version is free. Of all the social media assets I use, LinkedIn is the one that puts most pressure on me to upgrade to premium, paid services, but creating a free profile on LinkedIn allows us to add a list of our publications – which is great for promoting books. Find me on LinkedIn and create your profile. I don't go behind the scenes on LinkedIn very often – I set it and forget it, and update things when I need to. You may want to participate there more often, especially if you are writing something in the corporate/employment sphere.

Goodreads is great

One of the world's largest reader-reviewed sources of book information, Amazon-owned Goodreads is often described as 'Facebook for readers'. Until you have published titles, you'll only be able to create a reader's profile, where you can share your reading experiences and follow authors and other readers. I was a Goodreads reader and reviewer for years before upgrading to my author page.

My social media asset is better than yours

Many in the day-job world love and swear by LinkedIn, as much as creatives swear by Pinterest and writers cannot sing Twitter's praises loud enough. All platforms get eager, loyal followers who will sell their granny on the promise that if only you were on that same one, all your marketing problems would be solved. Try to move through this enthusiasm with a firm smile plastered on your face, accepting that not everything is everything to everyone. Choose your social media assets based on your interests, just ensure you don't miss Twitter, Facebook and Goodreads if you want to promote writing and books.

High rolling on the social network

People may try to convince you that social media assets cost money, that they need 'premium' accounts in order to be secure and give you a large audience. They don't. All online entities have levels. Just create the most basic, free social media assets and ensure that when they try to sell you bells and whistles, you either decline, or understand why you're saying yes.

Recap

Get your social media assets sorted, adding your usernames and passwords to your safe place for future reference. This process will take a few sessions, but don't get despondent! When you hit an obstacle, make a cup of tea and go back to it with fresh eyes. When you're done, add your social media assets to your Gravatar profile, that way, when you make that brilliant observation on *The Guardian* culture page, people will be able to find your full range of social media assets!

Writer, start online publishing!

IT'S TIME TO create your regular online writing program, the hub through which a world of readers can discover your writing and, eventually, your books. We'll also look at how to send each online article you publish to your social media assets with one click, and monetising.

Publishing with WordPress

By now, you should have all your social media assets (if not, skip back to *Writer, show off your assets!* You'll need them for the next step). You should also have your own WordPress account, which you can use as a classic blog ('web-log') or as a website with regularly added content.

There are many freely-available online videos on the nuts and bolts of publishing on WordPress. Make sure you find one that tells you how to Tag and Categorise your posts.

These form the metadata that will help your readers find you when browsing through search engines. Never publish a post without at least one category and a cluster of tags (no more than ten tags and categories collectively with the basic, free WordPress account).

As a rule, categories are like the contents of a book – the objective main subjects (e.g. 'performers'). Tags are like the index of a book – the subjective individuals (e.g. 'Judy Davis').

A word on WordPress

Just dive into WordPress. There is plenty to learn, but the basics are easy to get your head around if you're familiar with Facebook. You select a theme (the look of your site – there are plenty of great free choices). A WordPress account will allow you to blog (which at its most basic is a diary of sorts) but you can create a website instead. My WordPress account has a home page via which readers can navigate to different sections.

My WordPress journey

When I started my site, I posted once a week, and I have not altered from this path. I started writing posts about my journey as a writer, and these quickly included pieces about my writing heroes and performers, writers and visual artists who inspired me.

After about six months I realised there was a theme emerging: I tended to write about people who threw down the gauntlet at pivotal moments. One of the earliest and most popular of these was *Don't f%o#k with Judy Davis* which continues to attract great numbers of readers across the world. Now, more than three years on, this article heads-up my book *Pluck: Exploits of the single-minded*, which made it to No. 12 on Amazon.

I labelled my site 'The Complete Works', and over the past three years I've added articles that I published in my journalism day-jobs, so it is truly a source of all my writing output. Along the way, I altered my site's look, the content of the two menus (one at the top and one at the side) and over the past few months, I monetised it.

My online writing program

Is like my writing schedule: I have all my settings on 'achievable' and 'realistic'. Many people ask me how I remain so prolific as a writer. The truth is, I write a minimum of one page of new material per week, and one blog post. That means I am constantly creating and constantly selling work. If I miss a week of new writing, I need to do two pages the following week. This sounds like very little, but I have maintained this schedule through full-time and part-time work, for more than three years, and I have never run out of ideas (which I jot down as soon as they come to me – there's always a list to get though). I have also created ten full-length titles in that period, written for other online platforms, and created a readership. A little output, executed consistently, adds up very quickly.

A monetising moment

All online publishers will encounter the attractive-sounding concept of monetising at some point. Some bloggers shamelessly beg for money, while others are paid to write about certain products under a commercial agreement. I encourage you to give away plenty of free articles for a long time, because that will allow readers to grow accustomed to you, your subject matter, your publishing schedule and your evolving plan.

WordPress will host paid advertising on their free sites (or you can pay a little per year to have no ads) – you'll need to wait until you have tens of thousands of visitors to your site every month to apply for a share of that advertising revenue, or you'll need to learn how to self-host your WordPress site (as in run the whole thing yourself, from the programming up) to manage your own ad revenue. I realised very quickly how self-hosting would drive me nuts and impinge on my writing schedule, so I settled on another plan: to monetise my website via the products I sell on it, namely my books. Since sales of these products are hosted on other sites (such as Amazon, iTunes, and Booktopia) I don't need permission from WordPress to promote and link to them.

One-click linkage

One of the best reasons to regularly post on WordPress is that you can configure your account to send each post to your social media assets. This is done via the 'Publicise' function (easy to locate just above the Publish button in the window where you create each of your posts). Follow the prompts to link your WordPress account to Facebook, Twitter, Google and others. In this manner, my once-a-week article is sent to all my followers as soon as I hit the Publish button.

Recap

Decide what kind of online writer you are and map-out a schedule. Accept this will evolve over time and don't beat yourself up if you need to alter it. One great post per month is better than a crap once-a-day blog post. Create your WordPress site – pick a theme and start posting. The most important thing is to just keep writing and publishing. Five minutes after I published my first WordPress post, someone in America read and liked it. Get your writing out there!

Writer, find your style!

HOPEFULLY BY NOW you have started a regular online publishing schedule. If not, scoot back to *Writer, start online publishing!* and get up to speed. In this session, you'll probably be pleased to read we're going to start getting to grips with some writing technique.

What kind of writer are you?

If, like me, you started regular online publishing without much direction, it's time to start refining your style. To achieve this, analyse what you've written to date on your site, and the work you have written in the past. What does this work have in common? Is there a theme, or several themes? If someone were to ask you what you write about, what is your answer? If you don't have a response, it's time to work it out.

After publishing online regularly for a few months, I realised I was writing about writers, performers, artists and others who took risks. When asked, I said I wrote about creative rebels.

Check the menu

When you have isolated your writing themes, ensure you include these in your site menu (if you have created one. If not, you'll want to consider at least one site menu). Menu 'buttons' give readers a guide to what kind of writer you are. Most websites have a 'home' button (navigating the reader back to your home page), an 'about' button (telling readers about you, the writer) and a 'contact' button (allowing readers to get in touch with you).

Most WordPress themes will allow extra menu buttons, so use these to tell readers what themes they can explore in your online work. In order to achieve the best SEO ('search engine optimisation') ensure these themes are listed in your site menu buttons and your site categories and tags, as this will guide the internet to make your name synonymous with certain subjects, genres and styles. Your site buttons can be the same as your tags and categories, allowing readers to aggregate and read your articles in the same theme.

Over time, I have become synonymous with LGBTIQ equality, writing, politics and the arts, all through my site menu, tags and categories.

Keep yourself nice

As an independent online publisher, regardless of what you write about, you are now in the driver's seat of you own publishing empire. The buck stops with you. If you doubt this, have a read of my article *The Publish Button killed the media* (via the search engine of my website – www.burgewords.com). It's important that you take on board the level of responsibility you have in ensuring not only good quality writing, but staying out of trouble when it comes to publishing work in the public domain.

Think of the internet and the social media as an international noticeboard, and ensure everything you publish there is ethical in addition to being entertaining.

Tips on writing and publishing style

I have written a series of articles on different online publishing genres. If you're interested in writing general news and lifestyle articles, check out *How to write excellent articles*. If you're interested in writing reviews and critiques, check out *Critiquing guide for armchair critics*. If you're interested in writing food-related articles, check out *Eating your words*. If you're writing under commercial agreements, or you're planning to, check out *The truth about writing advertorial*. If you're planning to write commercials or commercial material, check out *The truth about writing commercials* (via the search engine of my website – www.burgewords.com).

The big picture about images

WordPress has sophisticated image publishing components that allow online publishers to illustrate articles in a variety of ways. Featured Images are those that illustrate an article on your home page and stay with the story's URL as you distribute it through the social media, but images can be inserted throughout an online article. Copyright governs the use of other people's written content, but it also protects the use of their images, so be careful about using images that are not yours, or not in the public domain.

Wikipedia and its arm Wikimedia Commons are a great source of copyright-free images (those that are in the public domain). Click on images in Wikipedia to check their copyright status, and use the image search facility in Wikimedia Commons – you'll be surprised what is free for you to use. Often, you'll need to attribute the photographer or the owner of images. Do this with a hyperlink from your article, and/or a caption. Adding your own photographs is best done with a watermarked caption/copyright statement to ensure others know it belongs to you.

Publisher levelling off

How are you going with your regular online writing schedule? Did you try to be too prolific, or weren't you prolific enough? I post one online article every week. That works for me. Adjust your schedule to make it achievable for you and consistent for your readers. When I am pushed for time, I dig into my body of work from the print media and publish something from years ago to give it new life.

Google yourself

Here's the fun part! It's time to check on how well your metadata is working for you, and what position your website comes in at on a Google search. After a few weeks of online publishing, I appeared on page 47 of a Google search of my name. After another few weeks, I was in the top ten. After a few more weeks, I appeared on the first page every time, and have stayed there ever since through sheer prolificacy.

WARNING: Computer algorithms are so sophisticated that your device will start to put you in the No.1 spot as a matter of course. This does not mean everyone is seeing you in that place on every computer. Try googling yourself from another computer for a clearer picture of where your SEO is at. Remember, publish consistently, ensure your online articles are sent to Twitter, Facebook and your other social media assets (your 'Web of Fabulousness') using the WordPress 'Publicise' function. For a reminder about the importance of this cluster of online accounts, skip back to *Writer, show off your assets!*

Recap

Analyse your writing to date. What kind of writer are you? What subjects do you write about? Isolate your themes and ensure they are reflected in the menu buttons of your site and the tags and categories of each of your online articles. If that means adjusting your site content, take the time to revisit and reset all your metadata. Google yourself to see how well your SEO is working, and ensure you're using copyright-free images.

Writer, you're a journalist!

THE INTERNATIONAL MEDIA industry is in free-fall with the continued sacking and redundancy of journalists. Our newspapers, magazines and television programs are full of what is known as paid content. This advertising vs. editorial battle is as old as the media itself, but when the boards of media companies no longer have one experienced news person in their ranks, it could be said the newsmakers have completely lost any control over editorial content. Even public news services are being paid to host advertising as news. It's for this reason writers need to start behaving like journalists. We can no longer rely on paid journalism to get our messages out there, we simply need to start doing it ourselves.

Be an expert

There are many names for 'experts', influencers, for example, operating predominantly in the marketing sphere, but increasingly impacting the editorial content of the media. These are the people called upon to sit on panel shows or provide expert opinion in sections of the media. They often operate as brands – a marketing-oriented phenomenon designed to create awareness of themes, words, images and products. As writers in today's media and publishing landscape, it is essential we take elements of these processes and turn them to our advantage. If you write a lot about the environment, for example, you can adopt branding strategies to focus your output in that field. Tweet and Facebook on environmental issues to your audience. Write articles about the environment on your website. Tag and categorise your metadata with environmental keywords, but know exactly why you're doing it: you are on your way to becoming an influencer in that field.

Keep it real

Influencers and brand adopters are not required to be shallow, purely commercial types. If you are writing and researching subjects that you love, becoming an expert in those fields will come naturally.

Write opinion pieces about current events related to your work. Publish reviews about new publications related to your expertise. This is all great fodder for your writing program.

Share the love

When you're ready, start to connect with other online writers and journalists – start with me, if you like – and talk about your work and where it's taking you. Be prepared to be asked to contribute to other sites – this is a brilliant way to spread your metadata around and can be achieved in a number of ways. Other sites can reblog your posts directly from your site (and you can reciprocate), or you may be asked if you'd like a user profile for another blog, to upload and publish your own contribution – a very common way websites accept contributions. Don't expect to be paid for much of this output, rather, come to accept it as excellent distribution for your work that will generate followers on Twitter and Facebook, which increases your reach as an expert in your field.

Citizen journalism is not for the faint of heart

One of the most effective strategies I adopted as an online publisher was becoming a citizen journalist. I wrote about the process in two parts – *Voyage to the new news world* (via www.burgewords.com) – a process which not only led to increasing my readership but to paid work as an online journalist. I offer a gentle warning about citizen journalism – it's very accessible, but also highly contentious, because it's being relied on more and more by established media networks as a way to attract free content, and professional journalists can be very wary of citizen journalists. I wrote about this phenomenon in *Stand up, citizen journalists*. Citizen journalism is a minefield for writers who are also activists (or become activists over time, through their writing, like I did), so it's helpful to ponder the fine line between reporting and activism, and freedom of speech. I wrote about this in *You cannot burn a mummy blog* (via www.burgewords.com).

Journalism standards

Adhering to some kind of personal or professional standards as a journalist is not compulsory, but in the online sphere, where readers lay waiting to catch every typo and piece of plagiarism, it's wise to follow some basics if you're just starting out. Check out *How to write great articles* (via www.burgewords.com).

Say no to naysayers

Large sections of the international media readership remain under the illusion that the content they read is created by newsrooms full of busy journalists poring over editorial schedules. The reality could not be further from the truth – newsrooms are mainly empty, solo journalists are juggling the jobs that entire teams once did, their hours taken up with meeting the advertorial agenda of management to produce the paid content in their masthead. Citizen journalists are filling the gaps, although whenever the readership complains, they often let off steam about media conspiracies and lazy journalism. Don't let any of that stop you writing as an expert in your field. You don't need a degree, permission or professional qualifications, you only need journalism skills, consistency and guts. Check my article on *How to write wrong* (via www.burgewords.com).

Recap

As a writer and published author, you're going to need to forge relationships with journalists. The best place to start is by becoming a journalist yourself. Work out what you're expert in, and publish quality journalism on that. Keep an eye out for other journalists wanting to connect with you – these are invaluable future connections.

Writer, spread the word!

BY NOW, I hope you're a regular online publisher, consistently uploading articles in your field of expertise. You have configured your website to automatically send your articles to your web of fabulous social media assets. As a result, you should notice you're attracting a bit of a following – other bloggers, facebookers, tweeters and social media users.

If you're somehow thinking that your titles will eventually reach readers without this process, good news, I am graduating you from *Write, Regardless!* right now, because this course is not for you. If, on the other hand, you've come to terms with the reality that it doesn't matter if you want to be a traditionally or independently published author (or life has chosen one of these pathways for you), the bare minimum requirement is this social media platform you're building.

The endless journey

Here's a harsh reality: the distribution of your work will be your task for as long as you are publishing. The job of informing potential readers never stops. Let me say that again: it never, ever stops. I recently read *No Picnic*, the autobiography of Australian film and television producer Patricia Lovell, the force behind the screen version of *Picnic at Hanging Rock*. Lovell's book gives a fascinating insight into the journey of the independent creator, and one of her memorable revelations was how the role of marketing and publicising her films was lifelong.

Decades after they had disappeared from mainstream movie houses, Lovell was still selling her creations to TV networks, foreign territories, and video and DVD distributors. Each phase of this required new artwork, marketing packages, and adopting new forms of communication. If you want to create, you must make marketing, publicising and distribution a part of your life. It will often take more time and energy than writing.

Doubling your distribution

You may have noticed that using the automated 'publicise' function on your website does not give you much choice in the wording of your posts on your social media assets. When sending them to Twitter, it gives you no chance to add elements like #hashtags to the tweet. This can limit the extent to which your distribution is operating, so here are some simple ways to boost the distribution of your online publishing.

Top Twitter tips

Twitter is one of the greatest shop windows the publishing world has ever seen. Embracing it takes some fortitude, because it's a shallow experience most of the time, but it is also what you make of it, in a maximum of just 140 characters! The first step is to come to terms with what #hashtags do when used correctly. For many on social media, they're a clever (albeit useless) way to underline your point. That type of hashtag looks like this – #PeopleCantUseHashtags – see what I did there?

Using such pointless hashtags will connect you with no-one, but adding #auspol to your tweet on your review of a politician's latest book will put that article in the pathway of thousands of political enthusiasts. #Auspol is short for 'Australian Politics', so you can probably guess what #qldpol and #vicpol stand for, right? Hashtags I often use include #LGBT, #MarriageEquality and #Writing.

To make a tweet promoting your article, simply copy and paste the URL of that article (the web address – everything that appears in the box at the top of your internet browser) into the tweet. Twitter will automatically reduce it in size to no more than 20 characters, leaving you another 120 to use in the tweet. Watch how other tweeters make tweets work – short and sweet, pithy and pushy, or just plain funny. It's up to you, have fun!

If your tweet gets 'retweeted' it means another tweeter is sharing it with their followers. Give another tweeter a thrill and retweet their tweet to your followers. Retweets are distribution gold.

Facets of Facebook

Walking the Facebook tightrope as a writer with articles to promote and titles to sell can be wearying. Facebook is free, but over time Facebook Page account holders have been encouraged to buy (or 'boost') posts, and as that facility took off, Facebook began to curate who sees posts on Facebook Pages (business account) and Timelines (personal account).

To counter this limitation, I often manually post an article to my personal Timeline at a different day/time in the hope that it gets a greater reach. Facebook keeps its functionality very secret, so no-one knows how the algorithms really work.

Targeting social media users

One great workaround for the Facebook algorithms is being able to target, or 'tag' people into your Facebook post. I use this function to alert some of my followers to an article they may be interested in, or linking to a business, such as a bookshop that is stocking my books. You simply type the @ symbol before the Facebook Page name, or a Timeline name (to tag me you'd type @MichaelBurge:AuthorArtistPublisher) and it creates a hyperlink to that Facebook post, drawing attention to your article and a providing a link to that business, a win-win for you and them.

Public vs Private

All posts from a Facebook Page are automatically public – everyone can read them. Posts from a personal Facebook Timeline can be set to public or private, as you're posting, or afterwards. If you want a post on your personal timeline to be distributed by your followers to all their followers, you need to set it to public. Keep on top of Facebook's regular changes to the ways its system works in this regard.

Social media etiquette

There is none, you must set your own standards. Some people will not follow those who don't follow them back (#TeamFollowBack). Others hate tweets and posts that seek to promote something, and blatant self-promoters get regularly unfollowed. There are all kinds of traps – getting blocked, trolled, overlooked – it's a minefield, and now and again you'll see some poor soul trying to 'keep it positive' on Facebook because they're 'sick of all the negativity'... LOL. Newsflash: Nobody owns Facebook! All you can do is stick to your pathway and not compare yourself to others – be aware that many social media accounts have purchased those 250,000 followers just so they look popular and relevant.

Reciprocity is free

Across my first years on the social media, I found the most effective way to use these systems is to participate and reciprocate. If we expect others to read our articles, we are rightly expected to read theirs. A little give and take goes a very long way. Now and again you'll feel the heat of a rampant social media abuser. Ignore them or block them, delete the mess they've left on your timeline, and move on. Social media fights are ugly.

Real life is still better

Nothing sells your message more than meeting you in person, allowing others to gauge your demeanour, enjoy your personality and your level of humanity. In addition to social media distribution, I encourage writers to put themselves out there on occasion (I force myself to).

Go to events – you can post Facebook content from such gatherings, or 'live tweet' from them to your social media audience (as a journalist would do), and spend time meeting people who may be interested in your work.

Recap

As you create your books for publication, it is important – many, including me, say imperative – that writers build a distribution network. One of the most effective ways of starting is on the social media, but it's just the beginning of a process that will continue for as long as you seek readers for your books.

Writer, don't lose the plot!

THE FIRST SIX chapters of *Write, Regardless!* are about establishing an online social media platform, something all writers need to be doing for ourselves long before we start the process of publishing our books. Think of it this way... once you've got the regular selling process in place, it leaves you more time and energy to focus on regularly creating. To that end, we'll start looking in more detail at the writing process, beginning with what I believe to be the essential foundation of all good storytelling: effective plotting.

Dig away at your plot

Every writer plots differently, but plotting a story is never executed just once or in isolation, it tends to evolve throughout the process of putting a title together. This article is something you'll probably need to dip into across the writing of your work in order to stay on course with your plot.

Plotting a first draft

I am often asked if it's possible to plot well in a first draft, and whether writers can keep track of where we are in our unfolding plots. The short answer is that I am a great advocate for belting out a first draft without focussing too much on plot. See where the inspiration takes you. There is a payoff for this rule-free 'luxury', however, which is that eventually we have to get tough on our plots in order to shape subsequent drafts. Having said that, the more we write, the more we become capable of shaping a plot in a first draft.

Second draft and beyond

There's no excuse for neglecting a tough plot analysis while executing your second and subsequent drafts. This is your chance to make your work engaging and entertaining. Don't fall into the trap of believing that some literary fairy godmother is going to magically appear and make your first draft perfect. Submitting an incomplete, unworked manuscript is the height of writerly laziness and nobody in the publishing trade is paid to make your raw draft into a workable book. That's your job. Luckily, there are tools to help.

Bite-sized plot structure

Depending on what genre and format you're writing, there is more than one way to plot a story. The archetypal five-act plot (check out *Plotting to win* via www.burgewords.com) is the classic structure for novels and can be applied to long-form non-fiction.

The archetypal three-act plot (*Great stories come in threes* via www.burgewords.com) is commonly applied to screenplays and plays, although it's really a truncated form of the five-act plot.

Remember, these are a plot's starting points. The rules are not there to break (if you want to entertain readers/viewers) but rather to bend. Your ability to be flexible with the rules is what will make your writing original.

Perfect plot points

Drilling deeper into plot structure will expose more detail on precise moments that heighten the experience for readers/viewers, such as the narrative hook (check out *The shit-click moment* via www.burgewords.com), the call to action (*The call to action* via www.burgewords.com), and the point of no return (*The point of no return* via www.burgewords.com). Don't complete a second or subsequent draft of your books/scripts without them.

Fighting the 'formula'

I've had many animated discussions with writers who don't believe in structured plots. I am not here to convince anyone of the need to plot their stories, but I do know that a joke has a formulaic structure (set-up, punchline) and a ghost story by a campfire has one too. Try telling such stories without sticking to tried and true plot structure will leave the teller looking as though they have no sense of humour. We all anticipate a punchline in a joke, and we know a ghost story has a chilling moment ahead, yet we submit to the formula without question. Plotting a novel or screenplay is no different, in fact these writing formats require more conscious plotting, since they are longer and fall further from the formula, especially if we seek to be original.

The *Hamlet* argument

Many plotting naysayers pull the *Hamlet* card, suggesting the Prince of Denmark's "To be, or not to be" speech by William Shakespeare is literature's greatest example of a character in some fascinating kind of stasis that gives all

writers an excuse to avoid plotting better stories. While
it's true Hamlet works himself into a state of not
knowing what to do, his famous monologue is actually
almost halfway through Shakespeare's plot. The play
opens with the unlikeliest of events – the purported
appearance of a ghost on the ramparts of Elsinore, and
on the basis of what may be an hallucination, the hero
drives the action through several major plot points before
he pauses, thinks, and wonders if it might be better to die
than go on. Sorry, plotting naysayers, *Hamlet* is not your
trump card, nor is *Waiting for Godot*. Great stories have
plots.

Create battles

When I get into a plot funk, I use a handy device to cut
the crap and uncover what needs fixing by finding the
'battle' in my story. All journeys of protagonists ('heroes')
and antagonists ('villains') involve conflict between the
two. They must get in each other's way. I believe
writers' reticence to structure these conflicts is the
greatest obstacle to good plotting. Name your hero and
villain, and let them do battle. If you miss this
fundamental core, you'll have no plot.

When plotting and marketing combine

Rare is the writer who has not fantasised about our work
in its finished form, imagining our books on shop shelves,
complete with our ideas for titles and covers. This
daydreaming can be an absolute writing killer, but there
is a way to spin it into plotting gold... although my
advice would be to try this process only when your first
draft is done.

Try it on for size

If you can't tell someone what your story is about, it's probably not well plotted. When you have a first draft, try writing a blurb of your work, the short taster on the back cover of a book. If this is hard work, it will show you where your plot is weak. If you don't know who to focus the blurb on, it's likely you don't yet know who your protagonist is. Not being able to create an interesting blurb for a manuscript is a sure sign it is not well-plotted.

Synopsis vs blurb

When you're approaching the point of submitting a manuscript to a publisher or a literary agent, or you're preparing to independently publish your work, you will need to create either a synopsis or a blurb of your title. A common trap for writers at this stage is to conflate a synopsis (an abridged version of a title allowing a quick analysis of its entire contents, including all plot points) and a blurb (a promotional 'taster' of the work which holds plot points back to generate interest). Writers need to reveal all plot points in a synopsis sent to prospective publishers and agents – let them in on your story's mysteries. Independent publishers need to entice readers by holding back some plot points (particularly our story's outcomes) when creating blurbs.

Case studies

During my research on the plotting process, I put a few well-known plots through their paces. Because the stories were not mine, the once-removed quality of the analysis made it easier, and I advise all writers to analyse the plots of their favourite books and scripts. My plot examinations of *Guess Who's Coming to Dinner* and *The Sum of Us*, both works of fiction, and *A Cry in Dark*, a non-fiction screenplay, can be accessed via the search engine on my website (www.burgewords.com). Try your own plot analysis as a way to grow familiar with the way stories are structured.

Recap

Structuring an engaging story by building a great plot is not something that magically happens in the editing process. It takes an understanding of storytelling that should be second nature to good writers. But have no fear, good plotting can be learned if you're prepared to be tough on yourself.

Writer, read your own work!

A FEW YEARS ago I asked my social media followers if anyone had complete or partial manuscripts sitting around, perhaps something potentially 'embarrassing'. This question yielded some interesting answers, and many fantastic potential books. One of the reasons I started *Write, Regardless!* was to assist stymied writers to dust these works off and breathe new life into them. The next step is one of the hardest for independent writers – successfully rewriting your first draft.

Don't send in your first draft... just DON'T!

The best thing writers can do with our newly-completed manuscripts is put them away. Ensure you have saved your work, backed it up on a memory stick, or at least printed it out, then bury it somewhere.

Unfortunately, the negative reputation of large sections of the independent publishing industry is formed on the back of writers who complete a first draft of their books one day, then hit the publish button the next. But just because we *can* doesn't mean we *should*.

The only way to achieve objectivity about a piece of our work is to leave it alone for a while. I'd recommend a few months. Use that time to keep your social media platform buoyant. You're going to need readers and followers, so start attracting them! Of course if you have a long-buried manuscript already, the time has come to rewrite it.

Do the work!

It sounds far too simple, but the best way to rewrite great second and subsequent drafts is to learn the discipline of reading our own writing. This is harder than it sounds, but it's become an essential tool for all writers in an age when editing and proofreading have lost currency. Even if you are gifted with the perfect writer's pathway – your manuscript gets picked-up by a mainstream publisher, and you are assigned an editor who lovingly massages your talent – you are going to be better prepared for this luxury if you know your own work better than anyone else. The only way to achieve that is to read your manuscript. *Do the work.*

Manuscripts must be fit!

Approaching traditional publishers with a manuscript requires several drafts before submitting. I cannot say it enough: publishers are not looking for problem writers. They don't have the time, money, or inclination to find a 'genius' and shape their work. Sending a manuscript to a publisher or literary agent is just the same as job interviewing and auditioning – you and your work must be on top form from the very first moment you have the ear of industry professionals. *Do the work.*

Don't overdo every rewrite

For me, rewriting is about seeking entertainment and distraction within my own work. I figure that if I cannot move myself through my writing, then I am not offering anything to a reader. When we embark on a first read, many hours of work on our manuscripts lie ahead of us, so it's best to avoid getting stuck in too much detail. We need to see the big picture of our story arcs, not worry about spelling and grammar at this stage. Insert notes so you remember things that spring to mind, but move swiftly through your read, trusting that next time you'll make it even better.

Be hard on your plot!

By now you should have a good grasp on what makes a good dramatic story arc. Detailed reads of our work are our chance to see where our plotting is weak. Revisit my articles on plotting many times as you reshape yours, and do your own research on story structure. My advice would be to correct plot failings as soon as you discover them, because there is no use trying to gloss over a story with, say, no antagonist; or a novel in which there is no conflict; or a work of non-fiction that does not have an effective resolution. Be prepared to admit your first draft is not yet complete, and go back to the drawing board. That level of honesty with your writing will pay dividends down the track.

Writer angst

I have written plenty in *Write, Regardless!* about practical approaches to writing. It's time to focus a little on the emotion. If you find yourself distracted, head in the clouds, missing appointments or late for work, chances are most of your mind is happily engaged on your plot.

Don't panic! Your family and friends will notice a change, very often they'll interpret your daydreaming as a form of selfishness. Confessing to being a writer can trigger familial panic (we're loose cannons in all rigid economies, we creatives).

Reading, rewriting and plotting takes time, quietude and headspace, and when we don't get these things, if we are *doing the work*, our brain does something clever... it takes over and does it whenever it gets a chance, such as when we wake, or as we are drifting off to sleep, or doing the dishes, or driving. Surrender to this process. In order to achieve your writing, you'll need to do plenty of artful dodging with loved ones. Expect the odd angry outburst to surface if you are a writer *doing the work*. What you're probably having trouble expressing is your need for headspace.

Rewriting short stories

The art of writing entertaining short stories is something most writers attempt at some stage in our careers. It's a unique form of expression that relies on being even more adept at plotting, not less. Don't confuse 'shorter' with 'easier'. Check out my notes on rewriting short stories (*Short cuts* via www.burgewords.com).

Read the warning signs

The independent publishing marketplace is full of advice and tips on how to achieve success. I've been gleaning great ideas within it for years, but one thing I have learned to watch for are signs of back-pedalling. While the rush to the Publish Button has become a tempting shortcut, I have read plenty about self-published writers who design their book covers before embarking on the writing process; who set-up marketing campaigns before fleshing-out their novel's plot; and quite high-profile self published authors pulling their books off the virtual shelves to rework them. They do everything, it seems, apart from sitting still and actually reading their own work.

Recap

There are many exclamation marks in this article! That means there is an important message you need to listen to: you are the first audience of your output. If you want to be an effective writer, you need to practice the art of reading your own work. All the secrets to improving your manuscript are on the page already, even by their absence. Read, read, and read your own manuscripts. *Do the work.*

Writer, resuscitate your manuscript!

I'VE OFTEN BEEN approached by writers struggling to keep a writing project moving, full of angst and desperate for a solution. Incredible as it might seem, this is invariably the point writers decide to show their work to a publisher, hoping that some clue will be found in the manuscript that will render it instantly better. All writers reach a point when negative thoughts come pouring in, telling us we must have been crazy embarking on writing something nobody wants to read. Often we feel the opposite, determined that our work is perfectly formed and needs no adjustment. When either of these extremes happens to you, it's not time to submit your work or give up... it's time to diagnose your manuscript.

Who is the hero?

Every effective story (fiction and non-fiction) needs a protagonist, someone to lead the action, to barrack for and relate to. This might sound blatantly obvious, but one of the main blocks to manuscript health is lack of a hero. Heroes don't need to be 'good' (they can be anti-heroes) and they don't need to be particularly heroic, they only need to be obvious.

What would *Gone With the Wind* be without Scarlett O'Hara? Imagine any of Bill Bryson's travel tomes without the author himself in the driving seat! Identifying your story's hero is the most important first step in getting a manuscript match fit.

Heroes with a twist

Sometimes, stories have multiple heroes, such as *Butch Cassidy and the Sundance Kid* which, like all 'buddy films', has a pair of protagonists driving the action.

Plots with more than one protagonist often have one hero take an outer (physical) journey, while one takes an inner (emotional) journey. A great example of this is *Thelma and Louise* in which Thelma (played by Susan Sarandon) physically drives the car and has strongly-plotted reasons for taking the route she decides on; whereas Louise (Geena Davis) is driven to an emotional transition in the passenger seat.

Protagonist teams (such as that in *The Big Chill*) ideally need to face the same conflicts (not strictly at the same time or in the same manner) in order to keep readers focussed on the plot.

Writers creating multiple-personality protagonists should consider either letting the audience in on the secret (as in *Superman*) or work the duality into an unfolding or complete surprise (as in *The Talented Mr Ripley*).

Protagonists in different time zones (like *Julie and Julia*) can intersect, but giving them complete story arcs of their own will create a more satisfactory experience for audiences.

Who is the villain?

All stories also need antagonists, those characters who get in the protagonist's way, but don't fall into the trap of thinking every villain must be 'bad'. Two of literature's greatest antagonists are Agatha Christie's Hercule Poirot and Miss Marple, who qualify as antagonists because they obstruct protagonists (Christie's murderers) through expert sleuthing.

Take Christie's detectives out of her novels and her protagonists would get away with murder, which is what happens in Patricia Highsmith's series of Tom Ripley novels, with plots tempered by Ripley's inner battle with himself as protagonist and antagonist.

In fiction and non-fiction, readers will smell a rat if the hero in pitted against a one-dimensional villain. A great test for a well-rounded antagonist is to ask yourself if your villain sees themselves as the hero of your story. Antagonists are simply protagonists on the opposing team. Both need to be equally three-dimensional.

Is there a battle?

Once you've identified your heroes and villains, you need to put them in the same arena and let them at one another relatively early in your manuscript. If you have opposing forces in play, your plot will have natural conflict, whereas if you keep them apart, readers will quickly lose interest.

Many first drafts take too long to get to the point of battle. Even non-fiction works need to reach a point of conflict to engage the reader. Check if your manuscript has a turning point around one-fifth into the word length, strong enough to create an ongoing battle between protagonist and antagonist.

Is there a winner?

You've spent months writing your manuscript, and you've taken the conflict to a certain point, but you can't seem to land your story. This is an extremely common plotting debacle, borne of not knowing if you're writing a tragedy or a comedy. Have no fear, there's a really easy fix: you just need to decide who wins, and it can only be hero or villain who claims the victory. Classic plot structure dictates that if the hero is better off at the end of the story than they were at the beginning, you've written a comedy. If the villain wins, it's a tragedy.

Ever since William Shakespeare invented the black comedy by combining the opposing forces of Greek tragedy and comedy, there has been humour in the saddest tales (think the gravedigger scene in *Hamlet*), and tears in the joy (think *Muriel's Wedding* in which Muriel's mother kills herself). Readers are waiting, just pick a winner! Your hard-won resolution will flow as soon as you do.

So your manuscript has legs?

If you have a hero, a villain, you've pitted them against one another and decided who wins, good news: your fiction or non-fiction manuscript will live. Before sending it to a publisher, there are a few more elements to look at.

Who is speaking?

First draft manuscripts often suffer from multiple viewpoints and perspectives, or 'voices'. Check that you've been consistent in your narration – there are several options for this which can be used exclusively or in combination. Narrative needs to be consistent in order to make an engaging experience for readers/viewers.

Where are we in time?

A very common confusing element for readers is time. If stories swing between time periods, or have subplots that take us away from the main action, writers easily let readers/viewers down by not giving clear reminders about where we are and who is who. Sometimes all it takes is a short recap of characters and storylines to keep readers in the loop of our unfolding stories, especially after you've taken your audience to another place for a chapter or two.

Equality calling

While re-plotting a manuscript, it's wise to run a few tried and true plot tests. One of the best is the Bechdel Test, which will show you instantly if there is gender bias in your writing, and should make all writers aware of the need to create three-dimensional female characters. The 'Smurfette Principle' serves a similar purpose, and the 'Russo Test' is a watchdog for written representations of LGBTIQ. Look them up.

Engagement

Plenty of never-seen, unrealised, un-engaging writing languishes when writers seek to avoid connecting with audiences. Some of us do this out of a desire to be 'literary' instead of 'popular', but I suggest writers come to terms with entertainment taking many forms, everything from distraction to enlightenment. At this stage of your writing, be as objective as you can and analyse your manuscript for sheer entertainment value. Will people want to keep reading? I believe your gut will tell you where your work is getting slow and boring.

The memoir muddle

Many emergent writers begin with a memoir project, often at the behest of friends who have encouraged us that 'there's a book in you!'. It's great to be supported by friends and family, who are our first audience, but when the hero of our work is us and the plot is the story of our lives, an extraordinary amount of objectivity is required. The temptation is to write a completely heroic version of ourselves and a totally villainous version of people we perceive have wronged us. An inability to see and record our own negative actions, and the positive actions of others, has brought many a memoir manuscript to a complete halt. If you think this might be the issue you're having with your memoir, have the guts to record yourself as a 'warts and all' hero, and seek the reasons antagonists got in your way. It will give you more material and make for a better read.

Recap

You've read your manuscript. Congratulations. Now it's time to get tough on yourself and put your plot through its paces. Get over all fears that plotting is a formulaic, restrictive process, and check your work has the ingredients of archetypal storytelling, the kind that successful authors have been engaging for centuries.

Writer, be a 'beta' reader!

ONCE YOU'VE READ your manuscript, ensured the plot is the best you can make it at this stage, and seen to any glaring inconsistencies in your narrative, it's time to have your work read by someone else. In the independent and traditional publishing landscapes, this is the moment to seek out beta readers, and for you to become one.

You can do beta than that

Beta readers are not family. Cousin Myrtle is not going to give you objective criticism on your manuscript, nor is Uncle Eric. They will always love everything you do, blinking in slightly confused admiration about your writing pursuits, but they are undoubtedly not equipped to read and appraise an emergent piece of writing. Beta readers are other writers or people who work with words (editors, academics, sub-editors, journalists, etc.). Want a house planned? Go to an architect. Want a manuscript appraised? Go to a wordsmith.

Beta currency

Often the stock-in-trade of writing groups, beta reading should always be about reciprocity. After telling people you're a writer, be prepared for other writers to ask you to read for them. I have been doing so for long enough that I've read second and third titles by the same writers, and vice-versa. The process makes you into a great watchdog of their work, and they provide the same essential service for you. Get used to regular beta reading – all your work on plotting and narrative sets you in good stead for the process.

One last read... for now

As a courtesy to your beta readers, before sending them your manuscript, give it one more read through to ensure it's the best it can be at this stage. This will invariably involve working on it more before sending it off, but hopefully you're getting used to the reality that being a writer is all about *doing the work*.

The term 'beta' reader stems from the second letter of the Greek alphabet, which assumes there is someone in the 'alpha' reading position. That's you.

Beta courtesy

When sending your manuscript to a beta reader, it's wise to lay down some ground rules. If you only seek feedback on plot, say so. If you want the whole shebang, through to spelling, ask for it, but also respect that a voluntary beta reader may not have the time or inclination to go into great detail. The format you send your manuscript in will depend on these decisions, particularly if you want to enable the beta reader to leave sticky notes or comments in the places they refer to.

The most important feedback a beta reader can give you is about the manuscript's readability (which is indelibly linked to your plot), so while it would be helpful for someone to proofread your manuscript, this is not the stage for it.

Beta packaging

There is no need for a manuscript to have a final title. The title is not important at this stage, although rare is the writer who has not decided on one, but be prepared for it to evolve down the track. Ensure your manuscript is legible. There are a number of formats to follow (the classic plain typeface, one-inch margin on four sides, double-spaced lineation, page numbers, new chapter-new page format is standard) but down the track you will be required to tailor your manuscript to different publisher's requirements.

Some beta readers will ask you for a printed manuscript, or at least some payment to cover the cost of paper and ink for printing it out at their end. This is an entirely reasonable request, and if that makes you roll your eyes, this is your first taste of the electronic vs print tussle of publishing. A very large proportion of the reading public will not read a book on a screen. Get used to it.

Beta deadlines

When selecting a beta reader, it's always okay to negotiate a deadline for their response. Most writers are keen to get their work to publishers (or to self publish), so an open-ended time period to read a manuscript can become a drag. Be real with your potential beta readers, indicating a notional timeframe. A month is not unreasonable. Six months is way too long. Give beta readers permission to tell you they got to a certain point and got confused or lost interest. This feedback is essential and shows you where to immediately rework your book.

Paid reading

Ever since the independent publishing marketplace expanded, manuscript appraisal services have been popping up in all major publishing territories. There is no standard fee, which is usually charged per word, and there are plenty of companies seeking to stream writers into their independent publishing services ('taking your book from manuscript to paperback'). If you're going to pay for the service, clear negotiations and a contract are essential, outlining costs, timeframe and what you're paying for.

Beta feedback

Reading the responses of beta readers is one of the most difficult stages of the writing process. Good beta readers know this, and do not seek to destroy the spark of a writer's soul when they critique. It's very important to remember that receiving negative feedback is really the point of beta reading – rather get it now before your book is a paperback sitting on the shop shelves, when the only way to change anything is to pulp the lot.

Sifting criticism

It takes years of practice, but it is possible to gauge constructive criticism. If you find yourself having several 'a-ha' moments when reading the feedback of your beta readers, these are the first things to take on board. The reason is they resonate with you, but they can also frustrate because, of course, your inner critic is saying: *You should have thought of that!* All constructive criticism will inspire you into immediate action.

Worse is not beta

Not all beta readers are fair. Sometimes, writer jealousy kicks in and unreasonable or unwarranted feedback is given to your work. When this happens, it's your first opportunity to endure a bad review (and they are coming your way if you plan to publish anything). It can hurt like hell and inspire you to retaliate, but my advice is to seek clarity about the criticism with your beta reader, if you genuinely don't understand what it means. Beta-reader feedback can be an ongoing discourse, and I reckon good beta readers are best judged on their willingness to have a dialogue about their thoughts and responses to others' work. When providing feedback on a manuscript, remaining observant for gems of genius beneath piles of dross is preferable to swinging a wrecking ball.

Beta planning

Sometimes, beta readers prefer to give you feedback on the phone or in person, so you'll need to take detailed notes. If you can't act on the feedback immediately, ensure you save it somewhere you can find it later. There is no requirement to act on beta readers' feedback immediately. Giving their ideas brewing time can help our perspective when working out the next stage of the rewriting process. You may have multiple beta readers – if so, wait until they have all responded to your manuscript before you begin reworking it.

Beta marketing

Sometimes, a marketing issue will crop up in beta-reading feedback. This might give you a jolt if it's cold, hard sales issue, such as: 'A book like this will *never* sell!'. Marketing concerns can be a frightening reality for emergent writers. It's early days when our work is at manuscript stage, but marketing is always relevant in publishing, so it's wise to walk the line when sifting feedback that refers to a manuscript's genre, length, 'place in the market' and/or saleability. Don't balk at a beta reader's marketing-style feedback, it can help shape the direction of your publishing pathway, although if anyone tells you your book has no place in a bookshop, remember that's been said about many very successful books.

Recap

Sending your manuscript to its first readers is an incredibly courageous act. Congratulations! You have come a very long way. While your work is being read, use the time to continue your marketing through regular online publishing, and consider starting your second book!

Writer, don't rest!

SO, YOU'VE COMPLETED multiple drafts of your manuscript, you've reworked its plot and tweaked its narrative, and it's been sent to beta readers to see about its readability. You've *done the work*. Excellent. Here's a list of things to be getting on with while your book is off your desk.

Write another book

Writers are always getting ideas, and the chances of finding inspiration for more books while writing one is very high. Act on that motivation by sifting through ideas for what's got legs. Now that you have one book being read, maintain your regular writing schedule by getting another manuscript down. You're a writer, right? Keep it up.

Second book syndrome

Invariably a malady of high-maintenance, traditionally published authors who find their creative well has run dry with all the attention, 'second book syndrome' strikes when writers have too much thinking time and allow their writing schedule to go by the wayside.

Instead of indulging in a round of writer's angst, a good fix is to just start writing again and never allow space for this first-world problem to get a grip. What better way to avoid second book syndrome than to have one written by the time you've published your first?

How's you list looking?

No book publisher in the world prepares just one title and focuses all their attention on marketing it. All publishers, large and small, release annual lists of titles. If you are heading for the independent publishing pathway, you'll need to publish a list. If you plan to persist until a publisher accepts your manuscript, you'll need more books in the pipeline, in fact their very existence may sway a publisher's view of your viability. Readers love to be loyal to their favourite authors. When they find you, ensure you have a list of titles on offer.

Get reading

Even better, beta-read for another writer, there really is no better way to see how plot and narrative work. When they say that good teachers learn as much as their pupils, this is what they mean: reading another's manuscript will shine a strong light on your own. Spend some time reading published books. With your new writing knowledge, you'll probably learn something fresh from an old favourite, or you may notice how the 'latest, hottest thing' in the book trade is not all that hot or new: maybe the writer is simply adept at good plotting and narrative, and found original ways of utilising established storytelling techniques. Reading will show you how far your writing has come.

Cards close to your chest, writer!

The great temptation, in this isolating, internet-driven world, is to tell everyone you've finished writing a book and bask in the encouragement your peeps are bound to bestow on you. There is nothing more dangerous for the emergent writer than this kind of public display. It builds an expectation of you and attracts the inevitable question: "So, what's your book about?", which you might feel you're prepared for, but it stands to take a chunk of self assurance out of most writers each time it's asked.

A brainchild is born

There are times and places to share the news of a book's birth. Join a writer's group and let everyone know of your completed manuscript (a great way to find beta readers); or tell select friends who respect your creative boundaries (but be very sure they do).

If you are planning to independently publish your book, you'll eventually need to make an announcement to your social media network, but now is just not the time, when you don't even know for sure what the book will be called. Don't confuse manuscript completion with the start of a book's marketing campaign. For now, just keep marketing yourself as a writer in your fields of expertise. Readers will assume you have books in the pipeline.

Extend your networks

By now, you should have a growing social media presence, fed by your regular online articles. During this process, you'll have naturally seen and read work by other writers, published in other networks. Set aside some time to research and send your work to these websites and social media feeds, particularly if they are linked to your subject matter.

Offer articles for free

The people behind websites and social media groups (who sometimes identify themselves as editors) will appreciate an approach from a writer offering free content, which is as simple as them sharing your posts. Some feeds will allow you to self-post while following a set of group guidelines; others will offer you access as a site author or 'admin', leaving you to add articles at your convenience.

Ensure your work is quality journalism and always has a link back to your website or social media assets, which will allow readers to find you, follow you and therefore access your published works down the track.

The value of your posts being published is not in charging per word, but in increasing your social media following: your future audience.

Review a book

Preferably an independently published book. Whatever path your writing career takes, the most generous thing you can do as a participant in the publishing industry is to regularly review books.

Critical responses are a great way to fill your online publishing schedule with content that reflects on you as a good writer and increases your reach to potential readers.

Check out my tips for good reviewing (*Critiquing basics for armchair critics* via www.burgewords.com)

Recap

In terms of announcing your book is in a complete form, less is more at this stage, which is the antithesis of the 'share everything' world we have made for ourselves; but your work and sense of wellbeing as a writer depend on a bit of containment at this stage. Focus your energies on creating more work and increasing its reach.

Writer, join your tribe!

MANY WRITERS STRUGGLE alone with the task of marketing. Writing an entire book is enough of a challenge for even the most experienced wordsmiths, so when we're expected to run the marathon of multiple drafts, then turn around and create a publicity campaign for our work, we tend to stick our heads in the sand and hope like hell that something about our work will render all marketing efforts unnecessary. Here's a refresher on how you should already have started marketing if you're writing a book, and the good news is it involves interacting with other people.

Marketing from day one

Write, Regardless! has one fundamental message on marketing: to sell your book, you need to be actively promoting while you're writing and packaging it. This process takes a degree of multi-skilling which is akin to juggling, but adopting it removes the terrible feelings of exhaustion that result from completing a manuscript only to find you've run less than half the marathon. Marketing starts on day one of writing a book, and, for as long as you want others to buy and read your work, it never ends. Break through this mental obstacle and you're halfway to an effective marketing campaign.

Accessing word of mouth

The simple act of one person reading your book and recommending it to their friends is the oldest form of

marketing in the world, and it's still (relatively) free.
Entire advertising industries are built on convincing
people they need to part with their money in order to
generate word of mouth, but the good news for
independent publishers is that the social media is built to
facilitate infinite word-of-mouth experiences. If you've
come this far in *Write, Regardless!* and somehow decided
not to build your social media web of fabulousness,
you've got a lot of catching up to do.

Going tribal

It's time to take your facebooking up several levels and
find your social media tribe. Facebook offers facebookers
a sophisticated search engine. Take some time to seek out
others who think like you. This could be political groups,
social networks, or book clubs... anyone gathering for a
common cause which relates in some way to the subject
and/or genre of your writing. Sometimes these are
closed groups, and you simply apply to join. Sometimes,
these groups allow participants to post without
permission, following a set of group rules and guidelines.
Other groups are managed by an 'admin' person or
persons, who you can send messages to, requesting
they 'share' one of your posts.

Admins have replicated the role that editors fulfill for
news sources, aggregating content for group followers,
and they are often hungry for relevant contributions.
This is where you come in, providing articles that relate
to, mention, provide extracts of and links to, your books.
Never do the hard sell in these forums. The soft sell is
generally more persuasive. Don't tell me you can't do this
because you're not a journalist: you are!

Tasting the spam

Platforms like Facebook and Twitter can be used autonomously by writers marketing books – you simply post material about your titles whenever and however you like. A small warning: many social media participants are wary of spamming; and you don't have to do much for people to think you're a 'spambot' (a non-human junk mail distributor).

Endless sales tweets or filling your Facebook timeline with posts about your books is a big turn-off for many social media consumers. It's the *social* media, remember? The emphasis is on being *sociable*. You can market like those who hand out business cards at birthday parties, sure, but you'll start to notice your number of followers dropping. Selling all the time is very one-note. Mix it up with content that is not about your latest book.

Branding like an expert

Independent writers can tend to overlook tried and true marketing tools, such as brand management. It sounds a bit cold and corporate, but writers who publish our own work need to keep half an eye on how it sits in the marketplace. Ever since independent publishing began, centuries ago, writers have published work in serialised form. Think of the success of Mills and Boon and Penguin Books as a publishing brands: readers know exactly what they're buying (and they buy it often) plus they know how much they're paying; there is a consistent look, length and format, and there will be more of the product to purchase in the future. Think about what you want to achieve with your writing. Do you have a series in mind? Could you visually link different titles with a similar design palette? Can you position yourself as an expert in the field you're writing about?

Reading the marketplace

It's easy for writers to forget about reading and consuming in the same marketplace we plan to sell product within. If we avoid bookshops and book reviews, we can quickly lose touch with publishing basics, such as the current price of eBooks and paperbacks, or the evolution of publishing genres and writing styles.

Keep your book-lovers' antennae attuned for shifts in the book trade, and check the date of online articles you stumble across – years have passed since it was claimed eBooks would knock printed titles into oblivion, a prediction that turned out to be incorrect. The publishing industry, like all industries, moves the goalposts annually. What worked three years ago may not work now. If you want to write and publish, join the publishing industry and consume.

Hiring help

For some writers, running a marketing campaign is too much of an ask. They decide they have neither the time or the energy to promote their own work, and they seek to hire a publicist to generate sales.

There is no standard fee for publicists, and the scope of their role varies, but expect to pay thousands of dollars.

Some believe this scale of fees is justifiable since publicists are effectively selling access to a network of publicity that they've built over many years; but, as always, the onus is on you to be upfront about the cost, the terms and the outcomes.

Do your homework and ask for references and testimonials before paying for a publicist's services: you may well be hiring someone who is an independent author like you making a sideline income. Always create a contract with a publicist, laying out the parameters of the agreement, and hold them to account.

Deciding what 'success' means

It's been my experience that independent publishing success means different things to different readers and writers.

There are few benchmarks outside the usual 'bestseller' lists, so it's helpful for independent publishers to set the bar for ourselves by deciding what we view as successful outcomes. For me, gaining independent reviews and mainstream media coverage for my titles means I have succeeded in doing all that I can to promote them in the marketplace. When I have placed my paperbacks with major city bookshops, I feel I have succeeded in putting them in the pathway of readers. Anything less, for me, does not feel like success.

Work out what success will mean for you, and keep it realistic and measurable. This will help when you're feeling challenged by what you have started, and I assure you there will be many such moments.

Recap

Independent publishers do not operate in isolation, we are part of an international network creating product for a hungry audience that is increasingly diversifying the ways it accesses books. Replicate what has already worked for that industry through branding and word of mouth. Join the club by ensuring you buy, read and review books. Participate in social media groups and networks, not just by promoting your work, but by promoting the work of others too. Decide what will make you feel successful, and share that with your readers – they love knowing when the risk they took on you pays off!

Writer, you must submit!

IF YOU'VE EVER really *done the work* on a manuscript in the manner outlined in *Write, Regardless!*, allowed it to absorb your imagination and your heart; lost sleep over it and swung from thinking it's the worst thing ever written to moments of confidence that it says something, you'll know when it's time to give it a chance in the wider world. If you haven't *done the work*, you'll be full of doubt about your manuscript's quality, tempted to ask everyone what they think, and so out of touch with your inner bullshit monitor that you won't know how to sift the feedback. Here are some tips about finding if you're ready to submit your work to publishers and literary agents.

Submitting season

In this digital age, it's never been easier to prepare your submissions and have them all done and dusted in a very short time. After a standard three-month wait to see whether the marketplace, right now, is interested in your manuscript, if your work has not been picked-up you'll have a choice: publish it regardless or shove it in a desk drawer and try to forget about it.

Publisher or agent?

There are plenty of pros and cons about whether writers need an agent. You don't need a real estate agent to sell a house. It's the same with selling intellectual property. Writers can research the various submitting opportunities and send our work in directly, or we can hand the process over to someone to do the work for us. The submission materials you need to prepare are the same.

The agency pathway

There are the standard agencies that list the genres they will represent; then there are writing programs that operate as agents by matching writers with publishers; and then there are writing competitions that serve a similar purpose. Whenever your work is being represented by a third party between you and a publisher, it's a literary agency-type process. Be under no illusion – the author pays for this process upfront with a reduction in their advance or the competition entry fee; or at the back end as a percentage of royalties. Literary agents are best treated like real estate agents: assertively and courteously, with everything in writing before the 'For Sale' sign goes up.

The shock and awe principle

I deal with the submission process by using a little military energy known as 'shock and awe', because it cuts through the crap. Writers can get stymied by business strategies, the main one publishers deploy being the 'don't send your manuscript out to more than one publisher/agent at a time' advice. The ONLY party this principle benefits is the person looking at your great book submission. They have removed all competition by making you afraid to call the cavalry. When I submit a manuscript, I send it to all relevant publishers/agents at the same time, and I give the process three months maximum. This is how real estate has been sold forever, by creating that critical mass all property sellers desire. Intellectual property sellers have no reason to think or act differently. Literary agents certainly don't act on this advice – they create bidding wars between publishers whenever they can.

Direct-to-publisher submissions

Right now, major publishers have open doors for unsolicited manuscripts, uploaded via their websites. Usually once-a-month, these opportunities have snappy names like Penguin's Monthly Catch. They require writers to have a formatted manuscript, a synopsis and a writer's biography; some idea of the target audience and similar titles on the market; a social media platform (don't say I didn't warn you about the need for one); some skill in public speaking and communicating, and a couple of contacts in the publishing/media industry (warned you about that one too).

Fab formatting

There is a basic manuscript style in the English language, which is generally a one-inch page margin, plain font, page numbering and double-spaced text. This is not publishers being picky, it's a format that is easy on the eye for people who read a lot. There are international variations and your state or national writers' resource centre will tell you what is standard for your part of the world. There are no excuses for writers who don't adjust their manuscripts to a publisher's specifications. Sent a single-spaced manuscript of 250,000 words when they wanted 80,000 maximum, double-spaced? *Whoosh!* There goes your book back into the slush pile! Make it legible, plain (no sample cover art by Uncle Brian), with a decent working title and give it to them in the format and file type they ask for.

Super synopsis

A synopsis is not a blurb on the back of a published book, taunting the reader with hidden details about the story, it must allow a publisher to appraise your plot at a glance. If you've *done the work* plotting your book, a synopsis will be very easy to write. If you cannot write one, chances are your manuscript is not ready to submit. Explain your exposition, rising action, climax, falling action and denouement, and do it in the word-count they ask for.

Brilliant biography

Publishers are seeking background information about you as a writer, not necessarily where you went to school or your employment history, unless these relate to the manuscript you're submitting. Write your biog in the third person, show them your stuff as a wordsmith, and stick to the word-count they ask for (are you seeing a pattern here about not pissing them off?).

Insider knowledge

Many submission opportunities ask writers to name a few existing books that are similar to ours. Don't get on your high horse and claim you've written something so original there is nothing like it in the history of literature. The chances are there's a few similar titles out there in the hundreds of writing genres. This is publishing industry shorthand to understand your manuscript quickly. You'll be asked to nominate a genre and a format. Is it a long-form memoir? Is it a narrative non-fiction novella? Is it a short story collection? Be real and be honest.

Screen-savvy author

Agents and publishers have been known to request authors submit audition-style videos to see if we are media-friendly. Don't panic! If you need to create a short audition video, you can film yourself on your mobile phone camera. Choose a quiet, well-lit but shaded location that prevents the sun directly hitting your face, hit the front-facing camera symbol and select video. Next, hold the camera up horizontally like you're taking a selfie, pause, breathe, and introduce yourself before reading your writer's biog in the first person while looking into the camera lens. This will make it look as though you're addressing the viewer right in the eye, and give you a confident air. Email or message the clip to your desktop, then upload it with your book submission. Keep it simple and keep it short.

The fast response

Be prepared to have an agent or a publisher interested in your work very quickly. Like enthusiastic house hunters, they can act fast if they want to get your work off the market. This is not the moment to tell all your other prospects your work has been picked up. No real estate agent cancels further inspections on the strength of an enthusiastic potential buyer... no way! Some publishers/ agents will ask for a few weeks to read and consider your work because they like the sound of it. If so, calmly tell them you have made other submissions, but say that you have not been offered any contracts. If they are genuinely interested, they'll get reading and perhaps send you one. If you need help interpreting it, contact your writers' centre or arts-law centre for advice.

Be cool about contracts

Good publishing contracts are not lengthy – they don't need to be. If you're offered a contract, it should never ask you to assign copyright of your work to another party, but it should require you to warrant you created the work you have submitted. You should be allowed to negotiate a timeframe to submit your final drafts, and you and the publisher need to agree on the date the book will be published. They can set a time limit (and perhaps a fee scale) on author changes to the manuscript ahead of publication. This is to ensure you're a proactive, organised collaborator... if you're a literary vacillator, you'll pay for the privilege (remember when I warned you getting to grips with plotting would serve you even if you're traditionally published?). The contract should stipulate an advance against royalties (which is getting extremely rare in publishing these days) and a royalty percentage of book sales for the author.

Silence is the new no

If you haven't heard back from a publisher/agent after three months, they're telling you no. It's not courteous, it's not commensurate with the effort you have put into submitting your work to them, but it's the truth. They have rejected that manuscript and you'll never know why.

Accept this and move on. Check out my tips on dealing with literary rejection (*A thousand ways to say no* via www.burgewords.com).

Having another go

If you're keeping your eyes and ears open to publishing opportunities, you are sure to find a few more publishers/agents to submit your work to while you're waiting for a bite from your first round. When I do, I always submit. If you have your submitting materials ready to go, it takes a few minutes and keeps another ball in the air in your juggling act. After two rounds (over six months) it's likely you'll know if you've had enough silence.

Recap

While there is still a publishing industry, writers who have *done the work* on our manuscripts should have a go and submit our books for consideration. Be efficient with your time by preparing your work quickly and submitting to all publishers/agents you can find accepting work. Follow their submission guidelines to the letter. Mark a day in your diary three months from your critical mass of submitting. If you have not heard back from any of your submissions, it might be time to move on and publish your work, regardless.

Writer, are you ready to publish?

FOR THE FIRST time, a *Write, Regardless!* chapter has a question in the title not an exclamation mark. If you've *done the work* on your manuscript, sent it off to publishers for a minimum of six months and heard nothing back, you don't need a call to action, you need to give some serious thought about where to from here. Here are some of the major questions to ask yourself before leaping into independent publishing.

Can you meet your own expectations?

So your manuscript has been rejected by multiple publications. As Julia Child said in Nora Ephron's screenplay, *Julie & Julia*: "Boo-hoo…" (spoken with Julia Child-like hooting). Don't let anyone tell you your hurt is invalid. Rejection sucks. When you've come out of your shell, it's time to ask yourself if your writing journey is over, or if it's only just beginning? If you envisaged your book would be published one day, it's now up to you to see it done.

Can you be a publisher?

Although it creates books, publishing is not a particularly creative process, it's a form of business. I suggest you read the Wikipedia entry on publishing and come to terms with the industry's two-pronged nature: production and distribution. One process does not stand separately from the other. It doesn't need to be a book-trade behemoth, but if you want to publish your book, you're going to need to start, and operate, an independent publishing business.

Can you meet reader expectations?

Publishing is a business because millions of readers consume books. Standing on the brink of a publishing venture, ask yourself whether you can meet their needs. This means researching publishing genres and finding where your titles fit in, which requires the ability to be objective about your work. Publishing your own books will bring you face to face with hungry, experienced, critical, opinionated, readers across the world. Are you ready to meet their energy with confidence in your quality books, books and more books? Many of them will hate you for having the courage to self publish, are you ready for that?

Can you meet buyer expectations?

Books are a consumable commodity, sold in units. It sounds obvious, but people part with money to get them. Publishers, and all the operators in the book trade, from publishing platforms to book distributors and bookshops (online and bricks-and-mortar shops on the high street) all deservedly take a cut of the ever-changing unit price of books. Positioning yourself at one end of this competitive chain requires meeting the expectation of the buying public and booksellers. It means providing high-quality book elements: great covers, memorable titles, sensible use of word length and serialisation, and providing books in what publishers call 'lines' – that is, a range of titles on an annual basis. No publisher in the world publishes just one book.

Can you work the marketing machine?

I'm really going to cut the crap and ask if you're prepared to be a pushy arsehole at times? Marketing your books will take persistence, guts, working the room, pressure, stress and being annoying. It will keep you awake at night and take time away from your writing and your family. There are millions of books out there. You are going to have to grab and hold peoples' attention through an ongoing marketing campaign that, for as long as you want readers for your brainchildren, will never end. Is that quiet, 'nice' person who writes like an angel ready to become a marketing demon?

Can you take it up to booksellers?

The book trade is enormous, a place where the agenda is dominated by the need to make money. How will you react when a bookshop hasn't paid you for those copies of your book a year after they've been sold? How will you respond when a bookseller calls for in-store publicity materials, and they want them yesterday or your book won't be in the shop window? When your publishing platform is tardy in passing on your royalties, who do you talk to, and what do you say? Booksellers are businesspeople, some are jaded as all get out, and others are too enthusiastic for words. Are you ready?

Can you meet media expectations?

The media, as we knew it, is gone. Social media is where the bulk of communication is happening, with the average Facebook account holder operating as a free distributor for the mainstream (or 'traditional') media's stories. In this frenetic, limitless arena, publishers are promoting and selling books in ways that evolve every week. For independent publishers, savvy use of the social media in not an option, it's a necessity. If you choose to become a publisher, you need to be presentable, professional, and immune to a certain degree of negative feedback about what you're doing. Lucky you've already built that social media platform, right? (Or are you still thinking it's not necessary? LOL!).

Can you work the system?

Independent publishing requires the use of multiple online platforms to produce printed books and eBooks. Many of these do not differentiate between established book publishers and independent operators. The systems are often complicated and frustrating for beginners, but they are designed to publish and distribute quality books that would not look out of place on a high-street bookshop shelf. Are you ready for episodes of tearing your hair out and throwing things at the computer when it says no?

Are you up for joint-venture publishing?

For many writers, the answers to many of these questions is no. Lack of time and skills means a better option is to seek out a joint-venture publisher, one of the fastest-growing arms of the book trade. Many large and small publishing houses have joint-venture imprints, providing publishing and marketing services to writers, for a fee, often with a spirit of 'sharing the risk'. As with all products and services, working with a joint-venture publisher means negotiating a sound contract with all parameters agreed before setting out. There is currently no standard of fees, but if you're seeking to hand the entire process over to someone else, you're looking at thousands of dollars.

Is a joint-venture all that?

Many joint-venture publishers provide individual services (proofreading, for example), while others seek to stream writers into buying their entire suite of services. If joint-venture publishing is more your thing, there's plenty of choice out there, but be aware that independent publishers have exactly the same access to the global publishing industry as joint-venture publishers. While it can be a great relief to benefit from the support on the nitty-gritty of publishing processes, don't be under the impression that a joint-venture publisher can deliver anything independent publishing can't in terms of getting your book in front of readers.

Are you up for vanity publishing?

Many writers seek only to publish a book for friends and family, not a role in the international book trade. This process is called vanity publishing and has been around for decades, delivering quality books for happy customers. Don't conflate vanity publishing and joint-venture publishing. Vanity publishers have garnered a questionable reputation for high fees, sometimes very high, so be cautious when negotiating the details of your contract. Never hand over money before agreeing on all the terms of the process, and certainly don't pay the entire fee before seeing results – part payments are best when working with vanity publishers.

Recap

The publishing industry, from the largest publishing houses to the smallest independent presses, uses the same publishing platforms as self publishers, and it's become harder to tell the difference when you see books on shop shelves. This increase in access only works for consumers when the highest standard of publishing is pursued – readers are not easily fooled by bad product. If you want to become an independent publisher, be ready for a journey that demands the highest quality work, attention to detail, and marketing energy. There are no more publishing secrets in the book trade – they're all freely available to everyone who wants to produce a book and find readers, but they must be used wisely and well.

Writer, build your book!

ONCE THE DECISION to independently publish has been made, it's time to enter the more technical phase of publishing. You're about to transform a manuscript into a book that will endure, a process traditional publishers employ teams of experts to execute. These are the roles you need to manage as you put your book together, and the choices you have.

Will you print or not?

A few years ago, many were predicting the end of the printed book because the stats for eBook sales were rising exponentially; but between 2013 and 2015 they levelled off. Many readers still want to hold a printed book in their hands, but some writers don't want the extra hassle of formatting and distributing a paperback, and are happy to publish eBooks only. Do your research and know why you're deciding on one course or the other. I went into profit on the basis of one paperback order from one bibliographic company servicing one major city's libraries. That cheque paid for all the set up, publishing and launch fees of four titles. Publishing a printed title paid off for me.

Your print is my command!

Not too long ago, independent publishers were faced with a tough choice when having their books printed affordably: Should I print 500, or 1000? Either meant having plenty of spare books around in the garage and giving them away as presents for years, when sales didn't deplete the printed stock. The good news is those days are over, with print on demand (**POD**) services. Basically, when a customer orders your book, the system prints one for them. No waste, no storage, no need to give them away. Large tracts of books, both traditionally and independently published, are now sold **POD**, especially when ordered online.

Your favourite book

One of the best ways I found to get my head around putting a book together was to analyse my favourite titles, then emulate them. Printed books have a traditional style, with pagination, running headers, and chapter divisions of all kinds based on a standard format with odd numbers on the right-hand page and even numbers on the left. Readers will expect to see your printed book in this format, which applies to fiction and non-fiction, so it's wise to have very good reasons for deviating from it.

How strong is your platform?

Independent publishers need to select an online publishing platform. Some recommend publishing on all of them. I stick with one, which gives me print on demand and international distribution for eBooks and printed books across the full spectrum of sites, including Amazon Kindle and Apple's iBooks, and the world's largest printed book-selling sites, including Amazon's Book Depository. I also get access to the largest domestic booksellers in my country. Do your research and find a publishing platform that suits you.

Feeling your fringe benefits

As independent publishing became more accessible, writers' and publishers' associations began to form strategic business relationships with online publishing platforms to offer incentives to authors publishing our own work. There are an increasing number of options out there for writers to benefit from significant discounts in exchange for annual membership.

The option I chose gives me free uploads on all my eBook and paperback corrections, of which there are always plenty. This has saved me hundreds of dollars, far in excess of the membership fee. The best of these associations also distribute great material about the changing face of independent publishing.

Decoding your ISBN

Used throughout the global book trade, from bibliographic services to high-street bookshops and online book sellers, the International Standard Book Number (ISBN) is a unique identifier for every published book. They should appear in the 'front matter' of a book, near the copyright statement, and in the barcode on the back cover.

Writers can purchase them directly from ISBN services in all major publishing territories; but shop around a little – they are generally more expensive to purchase individually, so think about buying a batch. Remember, no publisher in the world produces just one title, and your eBook and printed editions of the same title will require different ISBNs.

Asserting your copyright

Many writers worry a lot about copyright, fearing their ideas will be ripped off and plagiarised. Yes, it's essential to use the copyright symbol in your book's front matter, but ensure you also assert your moral rights over your work in a separate, one-line statement, then move on. There are several sites that claim to be providing free downloads of eBooks, and yours might make an appearance, but these sites come and go, and they never lead people to free downloads, they only spread viruses and malware.

Scanning your barcodes

Barcodes are nifty shortcut allowing sales people to scan your book and instantly calculate its price, with all information linked to the title's ISBN. Many publishing platforms supply barcodes for free with your cover template, but they can also be sourced from online suppliers within your country. They'll ask for your ISBN in order to create a barcode, and like ISBNs they can be purchased more affordably in batches. Some retail sellers, such as supermarkets, require unique in-store barcodes in order to stock your books, which you'll need to arrange if you want to sell through that channel. You'll generally pay quite a premium for this service.

Your entitled book

I have a basic message when it comes to book titles: keep it simple. Titles follow standard patterns, particularly non-fiction, which uses main titles and straplines. For example, *Questionable Deeds: Making a stand for equal love* has a main title that is lyrical, while the strapline (sometimes called the subheading) is descriptive. Be aware that overly long titles can be prohibitive in catalogues and listings, four to six words maximum is a good standard. There is no copyright on titles. You could, for example, call your book *Star Wars*, but that name has been Trade Marked for the purposes of creating generations of memorabilia, preventing its use without permission.

Your cover story

The most contentious part of independent publishing is getting the cover right. It's an incredibly subjective field and unless you're visually gifted and can operate design software, like Photoshop, it's best to engage a cover designer. If you're confident doing it yourself, sites like Canva are very user-friendly and allow you to create a simple eBook cover for free or low cost, following a template. A good rule of thumb is to use one strong image as opposed to multiple, competing images. Check with your publishing platform on what dimensions and resolution they need the cover uploaded at, and work within their thresholds. Very often they'll ask you to use your title's ISBN as the file name. When sold online, your book's cover will appear at thumbnail size, so ensure the title is legible, and the image works in that tiny scale.

Their cover story

Covers for printed books are best created using a template that your publishing platform will send you, which will be created for you based on the number of pages in your book (to gauge the thickness of the spine).

Printed covers are achieved using a back-to-front format with the front cover on the right-hand side of the file, 'wrapping around' the book right-to-left and printed on one sheet of cardboard stock. Publishing platforms usually require you to provide an ISBN to generate a template, although some platforms will provide you with an ISBN. The same goes for barcodes – don't buy one until you know if your publishing platform provides them with templates.

Getting your head around word processing

One of the most important considerations when preparing to create a book is to check your word processing software can manage to format and export printed book and eBook files. Generally, two files are needed for every book: (1) An exterior, full-colour cover file; and (2) An interior, black and white file of the pages. For printed books, exterior and interior files are generally both PDFs ('Portable Document Format') in which all information is locked into place on each page throughout the document. For eBooks, exterior files are generally PDFs and the interior files are generally ePub files ('Electronic Publication') in which all information is fluid depending on what device it's read on. Printed book files are fixed. EBook files are fluid. Get your head around that difference and you'll be way ahead.

You've been warned about disclaimers!

For decades, published books have borne legal disclaimers protecting the author and publisher from litigation. Generally, fiction and non-fiction need to be identified as such, and this is where writers are wise to ensure privacy is afforded anyone whose story they have written about by changing names, locations etc. For educational books, a disclaimer might be appropriate to protect you from reader expectation about learning outcomes from your work. Disclaimers should not replace a thorough analysis of the legal ramifications of what you publish.

Does your book size matter?

There are several traditional sizes for books offered by publishing platforms – there is no standard and no rules, but making a larger book generally means it will be thin unless your word length can fill it. Some publishers deal with this by using a larger font size to pad the book out. Refer back to your favourite books and use your publishing platform's printed cover template generator as it will indicate what width the book will be with the font size you have chosen. There's a bit of guesswork involved initially, but experiment with dimensions and font sizes long before you decide on the final book size. That way, you won't have to reformat everything from scratch if you change your mind.

Your local bookshop

Is your best friend. Go in and introduce yourself and ask if they stock independently published titles. They may ask you to manage the ordering and delivery of your titles, or they may be happy to arrange that for themselves, using your book's ISBN. Work with and support your local bookshop. Think about hosting your book launch there, it can be a win-win for author and bookseller.

Don't let deadlines kill you

Books take weeks and months to format, proofread, print and distribute. Give yourself plenty of time to achieve this monumental process. Don't, for example, set your book launch date in stone until you're 100 per cent sure you can deliver, and so can all the players you're relying on in the publishing chain. You're the boss, launch when you are ready!

Back up your files

Start getting into the habit of religiously backing up all your publishing files. Once you've *done the work* on your books, you don't want to lose it all if your computer fails. I still use a USB memory stick and it works very well.

Recap

Putting a book together is a major challenge. These basics are just the start of each process, and they're designed to get you across the major elements to publishing before *Write, Regardless!* starts on the specifics. Take time to ensure you have the right computer software for creating printed books and eBooks. Research publishing platforms available in your country and if they access the distribution sites you want to sell your books into. Set gentle deadlines for yourself, as this will be a steep learning curve. Get out your favourite books and see how they are formatted. Chances are, you can emulate them.

Writer, get to market!

AS AN INDEPENDENT publisher of your own books, you'll quickly discover how marketing and promotion takes up as much time as writing. Don't despair, just dive in and stay on track with these handy tips on planning and running an effective marketing strategy.

Get your timing right

No publisher in the world completes a book and then starts a marketing campaign for it. The promotion of a title begins long before it hits the online marketplace or the shelves in high-street bookshops. Whenever you need a break from complicated publishing processes, make a cuppa and turn your efforts to marketing for a while. By the time you're ready to hit the publish button, your marketing plan will be well under way.

They said *what* about you?

One of the handiest marketing tools is a bunch of quotes about your book and about you as a writer. If you've benefitted from beta readers, it's entirely appropriate to ask them to furnish you with a snappy promotional quote about the title, and to approach journalists you already know within your social media platform. Printed books are replete with testimonials about the writer's previous or current work, they give readers confidence in the author's abilities. Work some great quotes into your printed book's cover design.

Coming to you this summer...

In order to roll out an effective marketing campaign, you'll need plenty of support materials. Key to this will be your book trailer.

In just the same way as movie trailers tease audiences with forthcoming films, effective book trailers provide a taste of a book's content. Don't think a book trailer needs to be a Hollywood epic – many of them are as simple and subtle as others are bold and brash.

I approach this challenge differently each time, using the basic video editing software that was included on my 2010-model desktop computer. Keep trailers short, simple and evocative, and upload them onto your YouTube account. From there, you can share them on your social media platform. Book trailer services can be accessed online, but, as always, agree on all the contract parameters before handing over any money.

Who are you and what do you look like?

Readers love to know more about writers they admire. If you have not already included a biography on your website, publish one well in advance of your book with an honest photograph of yourself.

Author biographies are required by almost every online book-selling and bibliographic platform, so keep it short and consistent. Have a high-resolution jpeg of your author photo handy, at least 500KB in size, for when you are asked to send one by a newspaper or an online publisher.

Let them know all about you

Online book industry sites offer free author pages to writer-publishers, allowing you to share your story with readers, upload book trailers and aggregate all your books in one easy-to-see place. You'll need to create a page in each Amazon territory via their Author Central facility (there is currently no service for this on Amazon.com.au). The Goodreads Author Program is also an excellent platform, with plenty of book marketing tips such as giveaways and online discussion forums.

The world wants to know you too

The global book trade makes use of bibliographic databases to promote and distribute new and forthcoming titles to book-sellers internationally. One of the biggest is Nielsen, which has country-specific services in most publishing territories, but allows independent publishers to upload book entries for free via their international portal Nielsen Title Editor. As soon as your book cover, author biography, blurb and social media platform is ready, upload an entry onto this service with your publishing date (ensuring you give yourself plenty of time – my advice would be to make it at least three months away).

Getting your great metadata

Nielsen will send details of your book into global book distribution networks, so make sure all information is definitive and accurate. You can edit your entries, but they take days to update. This process will add to the web of metadata on you and your published titles, and raise your online discoverability long before your book comes out. Occasionally, bibliographic services will offer you paid extras, but these are not compulsory. They've operated for decades with traditional publishers but only recently opened the gate to independents, so their interfaces can be hard to navigate. If in doubt, ask for support via their excellent online help services, which can take days to respond.

Your browsable online bookshop

Long before you publish, create an online bookshop on your website, with cover shots, advance quotes, and an idea about when interested buyers can expect your titles to be published. As material becomes available, such as your book trailer, or finished sections of your book, publish extracts that can be accessed via links from your bookshop to generate interest and build buyer expectation. When your book is available, change 'coming soon' to 'out now' with links through to your range of booksellers.

Your book is ready for launch

Book launches and author tours are traditional publishing tools that put writers in touch with their audiences. Form an ongoing relationship with one or more local bookshops – many of them will host a regular program of book events for their customer base, and usually charge authors a fee to staff the event, offering wine and light food for guests. Go to a bookshop's event when deciding on how and where to run yours. The best book launches are not overly long or late, have a point of focus (such as the author in conversation with a relevant guest commentator, or a book reading) and a book signing. This is your chance to make a splash and sell a few copies of your book, but keep things achievable and realistic – it's tough to get people out for any event these days, and give yourself plenty of lead time so that you are not rushing your book into print. To get more value out of your launch, have it recorded, even on your smartphone, and create an audio clip of it to share with your social media platform.

Your brilliant book media

Let's be real for a moment. Really, really real. The media will take absolutely no interest in a new, independently published writer's book. The mainstream media has been blasted apart by the internet and social media and relies on free book-related content from traditional publishers to fill their pages. If there's anyone left in the newsroom to see your press release, they're likely to think it's not a proper book if a publisher hasn't picked it up. Getting coverage in national media is incredibly tough and may require paying a publicist, and even that is no guarantee. If you want complex and effective media on your book, you're going to have to create and distribute it yourself.

Getting into your local paper

A press release about you and your work, sent to your local newspaper, is likely to get a run, but ensure you include a call to action, such as asking people to your book launch, and at least one excellent high-resolution photograph. Don't rely on journalists to create effective stories out of your press releases. Rather, build the story for them, based on a strong angle. The best way to create an angle is to write a headline – 'Novelist turns tables on ageing process in new love story' or 'Writer's stories not short on suspense' – and then write a full article (around 800-1000 words) below it. A good journalist will build on your press release by extracting the series of quotes you have provided about your book and your work. Double-check all details in a press release before sending it – you'll only get one chance to have it noticed and picked up.

Your book featured in an article

There are masses of traditional and independent news sites hungry to publish content daily. Trouble is, they can't afford to employ enough journalists to keep up with reader demand. This is where you come in, as a journalist for your own work. Create a full-length feature article (1000-1200 words) about the primary subject matter of your book, positioning yourself as an expert in the field, and offer it to the editors of related news sites and blogs in exchange for a plug for your book. Don't rely on them to insert the plug – write a short paragraph about your book at the end and include a hyperlink to your online bookshop.

A guaranteed interview about you

Someone once said: "Send yourself roses" and I have a similar take on interviews. In today's media, there is a tried-and-true, easy method of publishing interviews with a question and answer (Q&A) approach. Celebrities are often interviewed by email in this manner, with the questions published above each answer, and you can do something similar by interviewing yourself. You get to set the agenda, so make it relevant to your book and explore how and why you wrote it.

Make sure you include a hyperlink back to your online bookshop, and send the entire interview and your author photo to blogs and sites that publish content about books, ensuring that you offer the content free in exchange for a plug for your book.

Once it's been published somewhere else, publish it to your own site with a link back to where it first appeared.

Your reviews are in

They're highly effective word-of-mouth, but if you ever work out how to get readers to leave reviews, please let us all know. You'll make a fortune.

Tell your tribe

Whenever you get an article or review published about you and your book, be sure to tell your social media followers by posting it on your Facebook page and the pages of any Facebook groups you're a part of. Make it relevant to each audience with a short blurb above the post.

Think about having a simple flyer or postcard printed with details about your book, upcoming and previous titles, and all your contact information, and hand it out to interested readers. I pop one into every paperback I sell from my home office.

At least one place wants your book!

As a legal requirement of copyright law, most national and state libraries must be in receipt of free printed and electronic copies of your new book. Send and upload these to them, as their catalogue entries about your books make for great extra metadata on you and your work.

Recap

The effective marketing of a book is an enormous task traditional publishers will spend plenty of money on, usually engaging a publicist to get the news about new books into the mainstream media. Independent publishers can have a very rough time of this process, since our books are often stigmatised as somehow not good enough. Courageously generate your own media in order to cut through the prejudice, and start the process long before you hit the publish button on your book.

Writer, format your paperback!

CREATING A BOOK for readers to hold in their hands is a craft. For independent publishers, it's a chance to lovingly nurture our manuscripts into three dimensions, but can also lead to much hair-tearing angst, so it's best to keep things very simple. Here are the basics you'll need to get across in order to format your titles for a print on demand (POD) service.

Processing your words

Whether your computer is a PC or a Mac, you'll need word processing software that can paginate a document and export it as a PDF ('Portable Document Format'). Apple Pages and Microsoft Word are the main options that come with most desktop computer systems. Tablet computer versions of this software do not have all the components required to format paperbacks, so be aware when starting out that a desktop system will give you more options. All word processing software has a help tool to assist you in finding answers to questions. Use it, or Google what you're after and someone in the world will tell you what you need to know!

Sizing up your book

Your preferred POD service will offer standard book trade sizes. Use your word processor's page setup function to set the size of your paperback (your cover will need to match this exactly). Every page of the document will assume these dimensions automatically.

Breaking your sections

Paperbacks are divided into three main sections – front matter (introductions, copyright statements, etc.), body matter (often divided into chapters), and end matter (references, acknowledgments etc.).

You'll need to divide your document into sections using your word processor's section break tool. These breaks allow the addition of page headers (see below) and sequential page numbering (see below) and blank pages where required.

Why blank pages?

Have a look at a traditionally published book. There are always a few blank pages throughout, sometimes to ensure that chapters start on the right-hand page, or towards the end of the book. A blank page in a word processing document is achieved by making it a section all on its own – it's just a section with no information on it!

Your front matter

Front matter is usually short and concise, in a different font size and style to the body of a book. Here's the place to include a short biography about yourself and list your other works. Your disclaimers and copyright statements can appear on another page with any cataloguing-in-publication data. Contact your national library about how to apply for this free information on your title, which they will add to their online catalogue, thereby creating more metadata on you and your book.

Your body matter

The best rule of thumb is to ensure your work is legible. Font size is not the only consideration here — make sure you have generous margins (check the minimum with your POD service provider) and the words don't jam up the whole page. Count the number of lines of text on one page of your favourite book and ensure yours is similar. Nothing screams 'self published' louder than an author trying to economise by squashing too much text on a page with small letters and margins.

Your page headers

Traditionally published books use page headers. They are part of a reader's experience of books, but independent publishers often leave them off. There are many header variations. Page headers that run throughout a book are known as 'running headers'. Usually, the author's name runs throughout on the left-hand header and the book's title on the right. Short story collections can run the collection's title name on the left, and the story title on the right. Look at traditionally published books for ways to achieve effective headers.

Your page numbering

In the English-reading world, a book's first page numerically is traditionally the first page of the body matter, and takes a right-hand page. This embeds odd numbers on the right-hand page throughout the publication. Front matter is either un-numbered or uses Roman numerals in lower case (i, ii, iii, iv, v etc.). Blank pages often don't carry a page number, although one is allocated for them sequentially. This is where section breaks will assist you no end. You word processor will allow you to tailor each book section with certain characteristics, including a check box for whether you want to start that section with new numbers and headers, or to continue with the numbers and headers from the previous section.

Your book has how many pages?

When quoting the number of pages in your book to distributors and your POD service, it will be the total number of pages in the entire document, which will always be more than the number of pages bearing a number. Add your front, body and end matter together for the full number of pages in the document. Your word processing software will tell you how many pages there are in the entire document.

Page numbering and your paperback cover

When ordering your paperback cover template, remember to allocate the total number of pages in your word processing document, plus any extras your POD service asks you to allocate.

This is usually required to be an even number, with one blank left-hand page at the end of the file for the POD service to insert printing information on.

If you alter the length of your manuscript, it will increase the width of your paperback and you'll have to apply for a new cover template and adjust your paperback cover design accordingly.

Your widows and orphans

In typesetter parlance, small numbers of words on a line by themselves at the top of a page or the end of a paragraph are as forlorn as widows and orphans. Invariably, as you begin to format, you'll come across some in your book and you'll need to deal with them by using your word processing software's 'pagination and break' tool to pull them back to the previous page or paragraph, or push more text across to join the 'widowed' or 'orphaned' words, leaving them less 'forlorn'... (here's some extras to keep 'forlorn' company).

When is an orphan really an orphan?

As a general rule, when the last line of a paragraph appears at the top of a page or a column, if it takes up less than half the line, the words are orphans. If it takes up more than half the line, the line can stand as it is. Very often, there is simply no way to logistically deal with widows and orphans, and you'll need to edit your work down, or add to it, to lose them. This happens on every print edition of a newspaper or magazine, every day of the week.

Your book styles

Looking at your favourite books, notice whether each chapter has a capitalised word or words at the start. How did the typesetter deal with a break in the text? Experiment with your word processing software to achieve the look you want with your body matter. Traditionally, the text in a published book is justified (lined up) on the left- and right-hand of the page with no orphans... (see how lonely they look!).

Your multi-format consistency

If you're planning to create an eBook of your book, the formatting will be different, and *Write, Regardless!* will cover this in a future chapter. For now, get into the habit of ensuring that whenever you make changes to your manuscript, you make them to each version: paperback, eBook, and any other version you have backed up. This is the start of being an effective proofreader and editor of your work.

Recap

When embarking on the formatting of your book, my advice is to work out the dimensions very early by pasting the entire manuscript into a document set at your desired dimensions and line spacing. See how many pages it will be (including front and end matter) and order a free cover template from your POD service. They'll get back to you, usually in a matter of hours, and you'll be able to see how thick your paperback will be. Make the adjustments you need in scale and thickness until you have your ideal final book size before embarking on any more detailed formatting. Formatting is a laborious, detailed process. Give it time, take care and remember to save and back up files regularly.

Writer, format your eBook!

COMPARED TO THE process of formatting a paperback, putting an eBook together is relatively easy. The key to understanding the difference is the 'fixed vs. fluid' concept. The content of a paperback is fixed – every page remains locked in place however the file is printed; whereas the content of an eBook is fluid – there are no fixed pages and the content takes the dimensions and layout of whatever eReader (tablet, Kindle, smartphone, etcetera) the reader uses.

The best place to start is to follow the guidelines provided by your preferred online publishing platform. Here are the basic elements to creating an eBook.

Adapt your paperback

It's crucial that your paperback and eBook editions have the same content, and one of the best ways to ensure this is to adapt your paperback word processing document into a second document that you can then export as an Electronic Publishing format (ePub) file, bringing the same version of the content with the conversion.

Be careful not to reformat your original file, 'Save As' or make a copy first. Remember, when you make an adjustment to the content of your book in one file, you'll need to make the same adjustment to all other files. This is the first step in being an effective editor and proofreader of your own work: apply all changes to all editions!

What do you adjust?

When you have a copy of your original document, resize it back to the standard word processing dimensions (generally A4) but leave all body text of your chapters justified left and right.

Your new ISBN

International Standard Book Numbers (ISBN) are unique to every edition of the same book, so you'll need a new one for your eBook that is different to that of your paperback. Most independent publishers buy a cluster of ISBNs because it's cheaper to buy them in bulk. Ensure you insert the eBook's ISBN in the front matter of your eBook file. There is no need for a barcode on an eBook.

Drop your page numbers and headers

The good news about eBook publishing is that you don't need to concern yourself with page numbering – if you've created a new document out of your paperback, turn off all page-numbering functionality. You also won't need page headers or running headers. Your readers' eReading devices will create page numbers and running headers within your eBook. Some online book distribution sites require you to nominate a page length for your eBook – use the page length of your paperback, it's just a guide for booksellers and buyers.

Breaking your pages

As with paperbacks, it's preferable to break your eBook into sections. Books are divided into three main sections

– front matter (introductions, copyright statements, etc.), body matter (often divided into chapters), and end matter (references, acknowledgments etc.). In a paperback file, Section Breaks are used for this purpose, but Page Breaks will suffice in an eBook document.

What's on your menu?

The main difference between paperback and eBook formatting is the functionality afforded by an eBook's menu, or Table Of Contents (often abbreviated as TOC in word processing). Most online publishing platforms require all eBooks to have a TOC allowing readers to jump straight to each section or chapter by clicking on that section of the TOC.

Many independent publishers find this the trickiest part of eBook formatting. The best way to start is to search your desktop word processor for instructions on creating a TOC for an eBook. They often provide a template for publishers to replicate.

Your eBook cover

Covers for eBooks are the book's front cover only, in 'portrait' (upright rectangle) aspect ratio. Your publishing platform will require it to be uploaded by itself, generally as a jpeg or a PDF, following guidelines about what size to make the image.

There are many variations on this sizing, but it's important to follow your platform's specific requirements – they'll make your cover work wherever it appears within their distribution network.

Very often, publishing platforms require your cover to be inserted on the first page of your ePub file. Word processing documents generally allow images to be 'floating' (not centred on the page) or 'inline' (centred on the page). Your eBook's ePub file may be rejected by your publishing platform if the cover image is not 'inline'.

Embed your hyperlinks

A great advantage of an eBook edition of your book is the ability to include hyperlinks for your readers, allowing them to click-through to other content, which could lead them to your other books on your social media platform, or related information, or other resources on your subject matter. The options are endless.

Exporting your eBook

When you've created your eBook document in Microsoft Word or Apple Pages, you'll want to see how it looks on an eReader. The only way to achieve this is to export it in a format that eReaders can open, and ePub is one of the most popular.

If you're working on a desktop computer, you probably won't be able to open your ePub file – email it to yourself and open it on your tablet or mobile phone. Check it for formatting errors, and adjust it as needed.

When you're ready to upload your ePub file to your online publishing platform, you'll probably need to insert the ISBN as the file name (check their guidelines).

Recap

Ebooks are generally easier to format than paperbacks, with no need to worry about page numbering or headers. You can check your eBook formatting by exporting it as an ePub and reading it on a tablet or smartphone, seeing it just as a reader will when they buy your book from an online bookseller. Take the time to make sure you're happy with the way it looks before hitting the publish button.

Writer, polish your publication!

AT THE POINTY end of independently publishing a book, creative decisions come rushing at us from all directions. The pressure is on to have everything 'perfect' and ready, but don't be fooled into thinking that's the way it is in the book trade! Traditionally published books go through plenty of trial and error on their way to bookshelves. Here's some tips about getting the look and feel of your book right, including the most controversial… your book cover.

Sense of entitlement

Writers love to dream up brilliant book titles that inspire our writing process, but we'll often fight like cornered animals at the very suggestion of letting those ideas go. After all, our books are unique brainchildren, so the names we give them are incredibly personal; but as a book is approaching publication, and a final title needs to be settled on, remain open to alternatives.

Revive the Thesaurus

Beta readers are often the key to great title ideas. They are invariably our books' first readers and can usually identify our themes more clearly. One of the best ways to spark title ideas is to ask beta readers to name a few keywords that came to mind as they read our manuscripts. Look these up in a thesaurus and you'll soon see there are many ways to say the same thing, using several incredibly unique words to do so.

Book trade wisdom

The international marketplace is the best place to identify book title parameters. Long titles (more than six words) can struggle to maintain visual presence in online book sites, although there are plenty of successful examples, like Mark Haddon's *The Curious Incident of the Dog in the Night-Time* (2003). Many successful series rely on a short 'master' title, like the *Twilight* series, allowing varied and often longer sub-titles. Non-fiction books traditionally require straplines, a form of sub-heading.

Title theft!

We all want to be original, but chances are there are other books out there with the same or similar titles as ours (there will be at least one other writer with your name, also!). There is no copyright on titles. Somewhere between accepting everything is unique but few things are original, your book will find its place. Don't call your American Civil War novel *Gone With The Wind*, of course, but don't stress about similarities with other books and authors.

Judging a great book

The overwhelming majority of readers will judge your book instantly on its cover. Googling 'book covers' will lead you into internet nightmare country: everyone has an opinion in this highly contentious space. My advice is to keep things very, very simple. Engage a cover design artist or work up your own cover on software like Photoshop or Canva. The basic version of Canva is free to use, with templates and very low-cost elements for sale within it (such as images) to make perfectly good eBook and paperback covers.

Keep it simple

One strong image, one point of focus. Less is more on an effective book cover.

Size matters

Books are invariably sold with only the front cover at thumbnail size on desktop or mobile screens. The cover image and typography need to work effectively at that tiny scale. If buyers cannot read your cover, or get something from its imagery, they'll keep looking.

Where's the edge?

Most online booksellers and printed book catalogues display book covers against a white background. If you want your cover to stand out, make sure it's got solid edges. White or light covers will tend to disappear.

A designer relationship

If you've got strong ideas about your book cover and can operate basic computer software, it's probably best that you design your own cover. Expecting to pay a designer to merely push buttons for you while you muck around with ideas will drive you both insane and cost you a lot of money. If you have no visual skills at all but you're excited by the prospect of what an experienced creative will come up with, engage a designer by agreeing on price, time scale and outcomes beforehand.

What to expect from a cover designer

It's acceptable to expect that a designer will come up with an initial range of ideas for you both to choose a general design direction from; it's also acceptable for a designer to argue their case with you – always stay open to ideas that come out of the blue.

Designing is a creative process, just like writing, so accept that your designer may come up with the winning idea at the very last stage of design, just like your manuscript takes best shape close to the end of the rewriting process.

Picky clients pay more

If you keep making changes, expect to be charged. Good designers accept there will always be some amendments – three free alteration sessions is the standard (and appears in traditionally published book contracts) – but if you take the piss, it'll appear on your bill.

What a designer will expect of an author

Time. Nothing great ever came from a rush job. Furnish your designer with complete, accurate cover copy (title, author name and blurb) that will not require any changes to be made; and a cover template (with your book's unique barcode).

Basic respect for their process should be a given, but it's unfortunately quite rare. You might have spent years on your book, so an effective 'face' on it will take weeks or months to get right.

Ebook covers

Your online publishing platform will supply you with the correct dimensions for creating your eBook cover, which will be the equivalent of just the front cover of a printed book (no spine, no back cover, no barcode). YouTube is a great resource for videos on how to use Canva to create an effective eBook cover.

Paperback covers

Your Print On Demand (POD) publishing platform will supply you with a template (usually with a barcode, if you give them your ISBN) based on the number of pages in your paperback document. Remember, the page count will always be greater than the number of pages allocated a page number in your book (it's got front and end matter, right? If you change the number of pages in your book's interior file, the width of the book spine will change and you'll need to re-size your cover design accordingly. Head to YouTube for videos on using Canva to create an effective printed book cover.

Brilliant blurbs

Everywhere your book is sold and marketed – online, bookshop shelves, bibliographic services, libraries – there's a chance to attract readers with a great sales pitch, and there is no reason to use anything different to your back cover blurb. When creating a great blurb, the best place to start is the plotting work you did on your book. Keep it short – it's not supposed to be a synopsis – and keep the reader guessing about your story's turning points.

Where's your proof?

The trial and error of independent book publishing will become apparent once you receive an uncorrected proof of your book, the culmination of years of hard literary work. Most POD platforms allow you to order one version of your title after you've uploaded the interior and exterior files. This small spend is your chance to save yourself hours of angst (and plenty of money) by holding one copy in your hand and checking it for accuracy.

Recap

The publishing industry uses many tried and true techniques to create books that look and sound great to buyers. There is no need for independent publishers to reinvent the wheel – emulate the book trade and allow your publication to seamlessly take its place among the titles available to hungry readers. Don't attempt a book cover design unless you're very sure you know what's expected, but if engaging a designer, it's still a good idea to get across the elements of effective book design to ensure the process runs smoothly. This is your chance to make your hard literary work shine!

Writer, show your proof!

BY NOW YOUR book and your plan to market it should be well advanced. You're nearly at the finish line with the formatted, beta-read manuscript that you've read multiple times from start to finish; your effective title and cover; all your publishing matter (such as an ISBN and barcode), and your established working relationships with the mainstream and social media into which to spread the good news about your book's publication. It's now time for one of the very hardest parts of the marathon: to proofread your book and ensure is passes the eagle eye of hungry readers.

Good housekeeping

What no independent publisher should try to do without is a cast-iron back up of their work somewhere external to their computer, such as a USB memory stick or a separate hard drive. Within that, ensure you always know which is the most up-to-date version of your work as you proofread it. If you're proofreading eBook and paperback versions of the same content, you'll need to ensure every change is made across each version. Work out what kind of system works for you, and stick to it religiously.

Copy editing

In independent publishing, beta-reading has come to replace what was once the first stage of copy-editing. After having your work read by one or more beta-readers, take the opportunity to use the feedback to rework it. Once you've formatted your work, and before you do your final proofreading, there is another chance to tweak your book's plotting and content. Be hard on yourself and make your book the best it can be.

Watch the formatting

Ensure that any copy-editing does not throw out your book's formatting. If you make cuts or a lot of additions, your paperback will end up thinner or thicker than it was and you may need to adjust the spine width of your cover design. Very often, a traditionally published book has a few blank pages at the very end. These are to allow for expansion and contraction of the content prior to publication without impacting the cover design, but check with your print on demand (POD) platform as it may have restrictions about leaving too many pages blank.

House style

Whether you complete your own copy editing or you engage someone, you'll need to decide on a house style or style guide. There are differences in publishing style between major international publishing territories that reflect not only the spelling of those regions, but also publishing conventions. Choose one and stick to it.

Consistency

There is no rule on earth that demands independent publishers follow an existing house style, but what readers will always notice is a lack of consistency in a book. Consistency suggests to readers that your choices are intentional, not mistakes. If your house style is all over the place, they'll be unforgiving. Staying consistent between books is also important. Think about visual links between book covers and interior styles across all the books you publish in a one-year period. Let readers grow familiar with your publishing style.

Proofreading

It's crunch time. If you want an excellent publication that doesn't let you (and your readers) down, this is your chance to prove yourself a quality book publisher with a future in the industry. There really is no way to avoid this stage of the process... put friends on notice, make the kids walk the dog, lock the office door, take the phone of the hook and put every sentence through its paces.

Contracting-out the job

You may wish to engage a copy-editor and/or a proofreader to complete this stage of the work for you. Agree on the terms of the job and the cost before they embark on the job, and which house style you require them to follow. Don't expect the work to be done swiftly if you want accuracy. As with every part of the publishing process, if you want speed, anticipate errors and an invoice that reflects your impatience.

Start at the end

After several reads of a manuscript, you're bound to have been alert to copy errors in the first half, and blind to them in the second. On one of your error-hunting missions, work backwards through your book, starting at the last section and working your way to the first, giving fresh eyes to text that's probably not had much focussed attention.

Mistakes on mistakes

One of the easiest stages to make proofreading mistakes is when you're correcting errors. Get into the habit of altering the text, then reading the whole sentence again to ensure you have corrected it properly.

Avoiding litigation!

As an independent publisher, it's crucial to ensure that what you are publishing does not defame anyone. If you're quoting a person or a source, check that you've been accurate. Be accurate with the portrayal of people's identity (job titles, spelling of their names, backgrounds).

If you are writing about real events, think about changing names and locations to protect the privacy of individuals, places and businesses, and include a disclaimer in your book's front matter. Be scrupulous about this process and don't rush it. Check every source, quote, attribution and reference. If in doubt about anything, leave it out.

Copyright clearances

If your work quotes from or includes the work of others, you'll need to get clearance from whoever owns or manages the copyright of the material.

Usually, your first port of call is the publisher of the work, who may seek clearance for your use of the material from the author.

Sometimes, work is out of copyright and in the public domain, and there may not be a need to get clearance, although out-of-copyright material is often held in a collection that requires clearance for its use (for example, an art gallery that owns a copyright-free painting).

Always check if clearance is required, or if there are limitations imposed on use of word and images; and always attribute a source where it is known.

Readers are your friends

Independent publishers need to come to terms with a reality: publishing without the support of others will mean making at least a few errors in your first print run. Even whole teams of highly skilled users of the English language have been known to miss obvious inaccuracies before titles hit the printing press.

Prepare for this inevitability by engaging 'first readers' of your work when it's just been published – perhaps your beta readers – and ask them to give you feedback about spelling mistakes, grammatical errors, inconsistencies, etc.

Your online publishing platform will allow you to make as many changes as required to the publicly available versions of your books. There'll be a few rogue copies out there with errors... but that happens to every book publisher in the world.

Recap

For many writers, there is a willingness to hit the publish button in a rush at the last minute, but quality publishers will slow down at this penultimate moment and proofread the work properly first. Let go of perfection and aim for consistency – imperfections will be picked up by your early readers, so invite them into the process. You can see the finish line from here, just don't trip!

Writer, you're an author!

THERE IS NOTHING quite like hitting the publish button on your own work. It's an even sweeter experience when you've been patient and really *done the work* on your book, confident that you've made it the best it can be with the resources at your disposal. Congratulations, writer... you have transformed yourself into an author! Here are a few considerations your new title brings with it.

The book blues

Many authors draw comparisons between publishing a book and having a baby, no doubt due to the long gestation period and the potential for a difficult birth. There's also a good chance you'll encounter something of an anti-climax after publishing a book, particularly after your launch has come and gone, and the initial flurry of sales has died down. This is a time to take great care of yourself. You've achieved something major after sending one of your precious brainchildren out into the world. You're bound to feel vulnerable as your work finds its feet.

Reviews (the good and the bad)

It won't take too long before you start garnering feedback on your publications, on online book-selling sites across the world, or social media sites like Goodreads. Be prepared for people to love and hate your work in equal measure. Bad reviews hurt, leaving authors feeling misunderstood and disheartened. My best advice on this is to let reviews be. Always encourage readers to write them, but read them very rarely, and never engage in an argument with a reviewer who didn't like what you wrote.

This is an incredibly difficult standard to maintain, and one of the best ways to get through it is to get busy on positive actions around your publications.

Keeping your book (and yourself) buoyant

The great thing about print on demand (**POD**) publishing services is that you don't have to sit with thousands of copies of your new book in your office. They can be printed in short runs, allowing independent publishers to plan marketing campaigns that are financially low-risk. Having said that, it's easy to end up with a few spare new paperbacks on your shelf. Get them out there!

Direct selling

Readers love meeting authors, especially when there's a copy of their book for sale. Reserve a weekend, gather up all spare copies of your book, print signs with great review quotes, and hold a stall at your local markets.

Ensure you have a special 'market price' for your book (such as a discount for buying more than one), and you'll shift a few copies; but there's an old marketing saying about never letting a customer go without being able to get in touch with them again!

Connect with readers

Direct selling gives authors an opportunity to begin an ongoing relationship with our readers. There are many ways to do this, such as handing out a business card, or becoming friends on social media. Starting an emailed newsletter allows you to regularly stay in touch with readers and let them know your news about upcoming titles and events you're participating in. Because avid readers still tend to enjoy the communication offered via email, they'll often readily agree to giving you their email address. Social media platforms like MailChimp can be used to create free or low-cost email newsletters for independent publishers, but always let respondents know you're not planning to sell or share their details with any third party.

Shameless self-distribution

Just about any bookshop or bibliographic service in the world will be able to stock or supply your book if it has an ISBN, but independent bookshops and libraries are likely to ask you to arrange for the printing and delivery of your titles directly. Work with them in their way and you're likely to shift a good number of copies. You'll also maximise your profits by cutting out the middle man.

Checking out the competition

An increasing number of book trade festivals and competitions are opening the door to independent publishers, who've grown from an anachronism into a relevant player in the international publishing industry. Some still have their gates firmly closed to indies and operate on an invitation-only basis, just check their application details and be prepared to travel. Many conferences, conventions and exhibitions are seeking authors to present their work, so think laterally and stay open to invitations.

Marketing madness

Selling stuff takes energy and an iron will. In this era, selling words in any format is in one of the most challenging periods in the history of publishing, as the social media inevitably supplants the mainstream media as the dominant platform for all things newsworthy and literary. Stay agile, take the knock-backs with a light approach and ensure you celebrate your wins.

In my first year of independent publishing, I made about one-third of the average income of a mainstream, traditionally published author, with absolutely no assistance from the media or the publishing industries. That left me feeling wiser but also, in my own way, successful. Remember that you define what it successful, not others. Keep to your goals and ignore all the white noise.

Adjust your course

Redesigning a cover, re-launching a title that has not been effective in the marketplace, and re-pricing or rebranding existing work are old publishing industry tricks. Independent publishers can benefit from employing all of them if we find our work doesn't hit the mark first time around. We can always think again, laterally and creatively!

Conceive another brainchild

As I have written on many occasions in *Write, Regardless!* no publisher ever releases just one book. One of the best ways to stave off post-publishing blues is to be already well on the way to completing another manuscript by the time they hit. Now that you know the process of independent publishing, achieving your second-born will be all the easier for you.

Recap

Publishing your first book, and ensuring it is a high-quality product that delivers for readers, is an incredible achievement. One of the best things you can do when you achieve it is to share the good news about how you contributed to making the world a better place for writers. *Write, Regardless!* is my way of inspiring wordsmiths to keep putting work out there despite the odds that traditional publishing poses. If I have inspired you, please find me and return the favour!

CPSIA information can be obtained
at www.ICGtesting.com
Printed in the USA
LVOW13s1740051117
555095LV00009BA/316/P